The Idea of Hindi
And
Other Essays

AF579255

Raman Sinha

Copyright © Raman Sinha 2024
All Rights Reserved.

ISBN

Paperback ISBN: 979-8-89610-948-8
Hardcase ISBN: 979-8-89610-949-5

This book has been published with all efforts taken to make the material error-free after the consent of the author. However, the author and the publisher do not assume and hereby disclaim any liability to any party for any loss, damage, or disruption caused by errors or omissions, whether such errors or omissions result from negligence, accident, or any other cause.

While every effort has been made to avoid any mistake or omission, this publication is being sold on the condition and understanding that neither the author nor the publishers or printers would be liable in any manner to any person by reason of any mistake or omission in this publication or for any action taken or omitted to be taken or advice rendered or accepted on the basis of this work. For any defect in printing or binding the publishers will be liable only to replace the defective copy by another copy of this work then available.

To the Memory of Alison Busch (1969-2019)

Contents

Preface

The essays compiled in this collection span a significant period of time—approximately fifteen years, from 2008 to 2023. These pieces were initially presented at various national and international academic seminars over the years. With the exception of two articles, all were originally presented in English and are being compiled in one volume for the first time. Naturally, these essays do not revolve around a single unifying theme. If there is any thread of coherence, it lies in the singular perspective from which they were conceived and developed.

Seminar papers are much like arrows aimed at a specific target; they are constrained by the necessity to remain focused on a particular goal. This constraint leaves little room for digression or exploration of tangential ideas. Reflecting on these essays now, I realize there were many thoughts and insights that were left unaddressed, overshadowed by the demands of brevity and focus. Revisiting them today, I feel the urge to expand on these unexplored dimensions. However, such an effort would essentially require crafting entirely new work—a task I have decided to defer for the future. For now, these essays are presented more or less as they were originally delivered, with the hope that they might prompt readers to reconsider established beliefs and, however modestly, illuminate some lesser-known or overlooked aspects of their respective subjects. It is my hope that this compilation will inspire readers to engage with these essays thoughtfully, perhaps even to question or reconsider some entrenched beliefs. No matter how modest or seemingly insignificant their contribution, I trust they will shed some light on both familiar and obscure aspects of the subjects they address. In doing so, they may open doors for new discussions, perspectives, and possibilities.

Reading through these essays today brings back vivid memories of the contexts in which they were presented—the atmosphere of the seminars, the audiences they engaged, and the spirited discussions that followed. I am reminded of the journeys undertaken to present them, both within the country and abroad, and of the joy of reconnecting with old friends and meeting new ones. These experiences, now firmly in the past, feel almost otherworldly, like glimpses of another life.

This book is dedicated to the memories of those vibrant days—the lively discussions, the spirited debates, and the camaraderie that accompanied them. These essays are a product of not just intellectual exploration but also the lived experiences of those journeys and encounters. They are, in a way, a testament to the transformative power of thought and dialogue. May this collection serve as both a reflection of those cherished moments and a catalyst for further inquiry and exploration by its readers.

Raman Sinha
Centre for Indian Languages
Jawaharlal Nehru University
New Delhi
2024

1

The Idea of Hindi: Past, Present and Future

The idea of Hindi has been one of the most contested and debated issues of the Indian modernity. One of the areas of contestation was basically the outcome of its ambiguity towards defining 'what is Hindi'? Since Hindi meant different thing for different people, it invariably led to the polemics pertaining to the question of Language and dialect, problematic of Hindi-Urdu-Hindustani, issues of Nationality and National language or Official language or Link language etc. Hindi is evolved and evolving all through in the process of encountering and to some extent, solving these issues.

What is Hindi?

A Language with Multi- Dialects or A commonwealth of Languages?

George Abraham Grierson (1851 – 1941), in his monumental 'Linguistic survey of India' (1903-1928). writes, "The name Hindi is popularly applied to all the various Aryan languages spoken between the Punjab on the west and the river Mahananda on the east; and between the Himalayas on the north and the river Narbada on the south. From these Bihari has already been subtracted. It is spoken in Bihar and the eastern districts of the north-western provinces. We shall also have to subtract the language of Rajputana, and there remain, still bearing the name of Hindi the dialect spoken in the basins of Jamna and the Ganges, say, from Sirhind in the Punjab to Benaras.These divide themselves into two main groups, entirely distinct from each other,—a Western and Eastern. The western include, amongst others, Bundeli, Kanauji, Braj Bhakha, and the standard Hindostani which forms the lingua franca of the greater part of India. These dialects are all various forms of one language, which I call Western Hindi. The eastern group includes the three dialects that together form the language which I term Eastern Hindi,"[1] The survey was based on the concept of hierarchically positioned languages with its dialects that became standard for later linguists and literary historian. In 1926, Hindi linguist Dr.Dhirendra verma (1897–1973) proposed a concept of 'Hindi Nation'[2] based on its dialects, ignoring the subtraction by Grierson of Bihar and Rajputana from the Hindi heartland, he writes: "According to 'Linguistic Survey' following dialects are being spoken in this area: Khari Boli, Bangru, Brajbhasha, Kanauji, Bundeli, Awadhi, Bagheli, Chhattisgarhi, Bhojpuri, Maithili, Magahi, Malawi, Jaipuri, Marwari, Garhwali and Kumauni.... there are lot of similarities between these dialects and the ancient provinces/republic ('Janapada') of this area. It seems, as if each province is a representative of these dialects in this order—Kuru, Kurujangal, Shoorsen, Panchal, Chedi, Kosal, Vatsa, Mahakosal, Kashi, Mithila, Masgadh, Awanti, Vatsaya, Marudes. There were no such famous provinces in Garhwali and Kumauni. This analogy with ancient republics, is it not a great attraction for forming a big

1 George Abraham Grierson(ed.), Linguistic Survey of India, vol.vi, Central Printing Office, Govt. of India, Calcutta, p.3

2 This idea was propounded first in an article published in the journal'shree sharada' from Jabalpur and later compiled as a book called Hindi Rashtra ya Suba Hindustan, published from the Leader Press, Allahabad, in 1930

state based on these dialects?"[3]This idea of 'Hindi Nation' based on its dialects was later developed by Ram Vilas Sharma.[4]

Hindi grammarian and linguist Kishori Das Vajpayee (1898-1981) in his magnum opus 'Hindi Shabdanushaasan' (1958), propounded Hindi in the same manner of hierarchically structured of dialects and language and proved that suffixes like 'Taddhitiya sambandh pratyay' 'ka' and 'ke' is the common thread running across all the dialects of Hindi[5] but later he modified his views in the second edition (1976) of this book by conceiving Hindi as a confederation or commonwealth of independent languages like Awadhi, Rajasthani, Brajbhasha, Bhojpuri, Maithili etc[6].

The formation of 'linguistic states' presupposes what is language and what is dialect but it was simply not possible to determine linguistically. This is one of the reasons why People's Linguistic survey of India (2014) opted out not to emphasize language/dialect distinctions in its survey. Chief Editor of this survey G.N.Devy pointed out, "Apart from the principle of determining language identity in terms of its relation with a given language family, the most ardently followed principle from Jones to Grierson, and beyond them, was that of the language and dialect distinction. I decided after thinking through nearly three decades and after numerous prolonged discussions with my colleagues in communities and within the PLSI editorial collective to avoid branding any of the languages as dialects. If a large number of people who speak a given language think that it is a language and

---

3 Hindi Rashtra ya Suba Hindustan, Leader Press, Allahabad, 1930, p.64

4 Bhasha aur Samaj, People's Publishing House, Delhi, 1956

5 Kishoridas Vajpayee, Hindi Shabdanushaasan, Nagri Pracharini Sabha, Varanasi, 4th edition 1988, p.521

6 Ibid, p.11

not a dialect, then it is better to accept it as a language even if conservative linguists may find the claim untenable. In any case, Linguists, while it has made impressive progress through the last two centuries as a field of study, has still a long way to go before it can unravel all the mysteries surrounding the behavior of verbal signs used by human beings for externalizing complex and abstract transactions. The question of dialects too is among those yet unresolved ones."[7]

This unresolved question of dialects becomes more vexed, volatile and acquires extra-linguistic dimensions when the whole edifice of 'linguistic states' and its electoral politics in independent India merges together. If we say dialects are independent languages the total percentage of Hindi speakers in Indian union drops to twenty six percent otherwise it is forty five percent, according to 2001 census.[8] in due course Eighth schedule of the constitution, which shows language's independent status in the Indian state became a battle ground — As per Articles 344(1) and 351 of the Indian Constitution, 14 were initially included in the Constitution. Sindhi language was added in 1967. Thereafter three more languages viz., Konkani, Manipuri and Nepali were included in 1992. Subsequently Bodo, Dogri, Maithili and Santhali were added in 2004. Now it is twenty two.[9] At present, as per Ministry of Home Affairs, there are demands for inclusion of 38 more languages in

---

7 People's Linguistic Survey of India, Vol.one, Orient Blacks Swan Pvt.Ltd. Delhi, First published, 2014, p.14

8 http://scroll.in/article/667570/read-the-fine-print-hindi-is-the-mother-tongue-of-only-26-per-cent-of-indians (accessed on 19.12. 2016)

9 Assamese, Bengali, Bodo, Dogri, Gujarati, Hindi, Kannada, Kashmiri, Konkani, Maithili, Malayalam, Manipuri, Marathi, Nepali, Odia, Punjabi, Sanskrit, Santhali, Sindhi, Tamil, Telugu, Urdu.

the Eighth Schedule to the Constitution, in which ten languages are from Hindi common wealth, these are :Angika, Bazika, Bhojpuri, Bundelkhandi, Magahi, Rajasthani, Chhattisgarhi, Garhwali (Pahari), Kumauni,, Pahari (Himachali)[10]. Now if these demands get fulfilled that is in the realm of populist politics and therefore non-academic it is anybody's guess what will happen to the idea of Hindi.

Status of Hindi: Declining or Evolving?

To determine the status of a language at any given point of time, one has to consider on two counts—-first its constitutional status, what 'law of the land', i.e. constitution of the country codifies and second, how it really appears, its presence on various levels of nation's life. First, let us see what constitution of India says—- Article 343.reads like this: "(1) The official language of the Union shall be Hindi in Devanagari script. (2) Not withstanding anything in clause (1), for a period of fifteen years from the commencement of this Constitution, the English language shall continue to be used for all the official purposes of the Union for which it was being used immediately before such commencement."[11] And again in Article 351 clearly gives directive for the development of Hindi language in these words: " It shall be the duty of the Union to promote the spread of the Hindi language, to develop it so that it may serve as a medium of expression for all the elements of the composite culture of India and to secure its enrichment by assimilating without interfering with its genius, the forms, style and expressions used

---

10 http://pib.nic.in/newsite/PrintRelease.aspx?relid=108051 (Accessed on 20.12.2016)

11 The Constitution of India, Govvernment of India, Ministry of Law and Justice (Legislative Department), New Delhi, 2015 pp.218

in Hindustani and in the other languages of India specified in the Eighth Schedule, and by drawing, wherever necessary or desirable, for its vocabulary, primarily on Sanskrit and secondarily on other languages."[12]

It is debatable whether Indian state has been successful in charging its duty as expected in article 351 or not but it is a fact that Hindi as official language (Rajbhasha) miserably failed to replace English that is still continuing for all the official purposes of the union, forget about fifteen years even after sixty six years of commencement of the Constitution. It seems that constitution of India perceived Hindi as official language (not sole but co. along with English) but expected from it to fulfill the duty of a National language. So the duty was disproportionate to what rights were assured by the constitution, even then Hindi has been very successful in linking the whole nation. Even in 1968, Baldev Raj Nair noted that "There is some evidence that when people from different regions, not familiar with English, interact over a period of time, it is Hindi that emerges among them as the link language, even when some of them did not know it to begin with" and he concluded by saying that, "Several social forces, regardless of any initiative on the part of the Central Government, seem to be working for the greater spread of Hindi as a link language. The very large size of the Hindi-speaking population constitutes an attractive market for a variety of goods and services, and is likely to propel people into a familiarity with the language in order to take advantage of this market."[13] If you compare the size and reach of the sixties market of

---

12 Ibid, pp.222-223

13 Economic and Political Weekly, Vol. 3, No. 6 (Feb. 10, 1968), pp. 297-305 Stable URL:http://www.jstor.org/stable/4358239, Accessed on 14-11-2016 17:42 UTC

planned economy with today's open market of liberalized economy, the need 'to take advantage of this market' has grown manifold. It is no coincidence that now the global growth rate of Hindi appears to have outpaced the global growth of English[14] As it is reported, "according to the 2006 National Readership Survey(NRS), there is not a single English-language newspaper in the top ten in terms of readership. The *Times of India* the largest English-language newspaper figured at number 11, with a readership of 7.4 million, while *Dainik Jagran* and *Dainik Bhaskar the* top two Hindi newspapers, have readership base of 21.16 and 20.95 million respectively. Similarly, the NRS 2006 reported that vernacular dailies have grown from 191 million readers to 203.6 million, while English-language dailies have stagnated at around 21 million."[15] It could not be primarily the outcome of Hindi speaking population growth, as it was suggested by some experts but there is no denying of facts that India's throbbing media and entertainment (M&E) industry with more than 600 television channels, 100 million pay-TV households, 70, 000 newspapers and 1, 000 films produced annually, its theatrical admissions around 3 billion[16], definitely has an recurring massive impact.

---

14 "Over the last 50 years, the world's Hindi-speaking population has increased from 260 million to 420 million. Over the same period, the English speaking population has gone from 320 million to 480 million. These figures indicate only those who say English is their mother tongue. It does not include those who speak English for professional use as a second language," said Ganesh Devy, Professor & Chair, PLSI.(http://www.indiaspend.com/cover-story/hindi-outpaces-english-globally-linguistic-survey-68309 accessed on 19.12.2016)

15 http://www.academia.edu/377215/Cultural_imperialism_or_vernacular_modernity_Hindi_newspapers_in_a_globalizing_India

16 http://indiainbusiness.nic.in/newdesign/upload/news/New_Horizons_Final.pdf (accessed on 22.12.2016)

This impact can be understood by the simple fact that when in 2012 star sports introduced Hindi commentary with the likes of Sunil Gavaskar, Kapil Dev, Navjot Singh Siddhu, Wasim Akram, Rameez Raja, not only it proved the futility and irrationality of 'house-divided' (Hindi-Urdu) but also the power of its combined commercial viability as it was reported that,"71 per cent of the viewership for the dual language-feed India-Australia series came from Hindi commentary."[17] "With this success India's first 24X7 Hindi sports channel, Star Sports 3, with content, graphics and shows in Hindi was launched in 2013 that is also providing Hindi commentary feed for the Indian Badminton League (IBL), Barclays Premier League (BPL) and Hockey India League (HIL) also. The same story was repeated when Sony Six had started commentary in Hindi for Pepsi IPL 2013 and suddenly their viewership reached close to 100 million.[18]

Film and cricket are two primary pillars of the Indian 'Culture-Industry' and It is noteworthy in this connection that "in the last two decades, the Indian Hindi film industry regularized what it attempted for the first time in 1994 with the film *Hum Aapke Hain Kaun* (Who am I to you), followed by *Dilwale Dulhania Le Jayenge* (People with heart will take away the bride) creating box office histories in the US, the UK and the Middle East. In 2007, in the UK, 14 out of the top 20 foreign films were Indian. These were part of a total of 69 Indian films that constituted 13.7% of all releases. On the television front, Zee started in 1995 in Africa and Europe, reaching US in 1998, and in 2001, to the Middle East

---

17 http://indiasportstv.blogspot.in/2014/02/71-percent-viewers-watched-spor

18 ibidhttp://indiainbusiness.nic.in/newdesign/upload/news/New_Horizons_Final.pdf (accessed on 22.12.2016)

and Asia Pacific. The USD 397 million Zee Group is one of India's first and largest integrated media and entertainment companies. It is also by far the biggest Indian TV player in the overseas market, with over four million subscribers and having 40% of its revenues from its overseas operations. Balaji telefilms, an Indian content provider, having produced 13, 000 hours of programming in five languages over last 12 years, created assembly-line production processes, a reality in the Indian television front...In the Internet space, Rajshri.com was launched in November 2006 along with the release of the blockbuster movie *Vivah* simultaneously in theatres and online – a first for the film industry worldwide. After 9 months, *Vivah* had been downloaded 6, 500 times at USD 10 each, most of it by the international audiences."[19] In short, it may be interpreted that Hindi is gradually becoming global.

It is true that Hindi is not the language of power and status in Modern India, whether it aspires for it or not that is another issue but to infer from this that it is declining[20], is not true.

In fact it is growing. The idea of Hindi cannot be institutionalized as Rajbhasha Vibhag (official language) tried to do or standardized as Mahavir Prasad Dwevedi (1864-1938) once attempted to do since it has been branching out in so many directions —in the east, in the west, in the south, in the north, in the overseas reflecting all its distinct colours in films, in TVs, in Radios in literatures, in cricket commentaries in media, in almost all walk of life as it is diversifying and simultaneously growing, it is evolving.

19 http://www.indianjournals.com/ijor.aspx?target=ijor:jgc&volume=6&issue =1&article=007(accessedon22.12.2016)

20 Hindustani in India, Anirudh Deshpande, Economic and Political Weekly, Vol. 35, No. 15 (Apr. 8-14, 2000), pp. 1240-1242

2

The Relevance of Indian Poetics

While pondering over the question of relevance in literature, Nirmal Verma has written that "If we look carefully, we will find that the word 'relevance' itself smells of time. The time that is today, we are today, we are who we are today – whatever you may say, the relevance of any artwork, no matter how old it is, is judged on the basis of how much it is able to illuminate the 'I' stuck at this moment in the infinite flow of time. In other words, this question is asked at the root of relevance, whether any artwork has so much power, so much capability, so much all-round richness in itself that it can rise above the specific circumstances of its time and 'jump' and reach our time? Time flows. The past has been left far behind. In this continuously flowing, constantly changing context of history, an artwork can be relevant to me today only in one sense (there is no other sense) that it Once again, at the tip of the entire history — with all its urgency, concentration and intensity can awaken my face of today within me and ask — who am I?[21]

If the 'I' in this quote is considered to be the work and the artwork as literary theory or poetics, then can it be claimed that Indian poetics can 'rise above the specific circumstances of its time' and 'jump' 'on the edge of the entire history once again — with all its immediacy, concentration and intensity' awaken the

21 Nirmal Verma, Kala ka Jokhim, Rajkamal Prakashan, Delhi, 2nd Edition, 1984, pp.39-40

contemporary writings and ask who it is? The test of the ability to raise this fundamental question began in the nineteenth century when the sensibility of the era changed under Western influence and genres like novel, short story, essay and even modern prose drama started emerging in Indian languages. To understand, explain and evaluate this new literature, North India had Sanskrit poetics — from *Natyashastra* to *Ras-Gangadhar* — and the *Lakshan Granthas* of the Braj Bhasha developed under its shadow, while on the other hand, the South had Tamil's Tolkappiyam. In the nineteenth century, leaving aside the *Lakshan Granthas* of Braj Bhasha, the original Sanskrit works on poetics were translated into English and into major Indian languages and along with it the business of critical analysis and evaluation started which is still going on and in which both Indian and Western scholars have been involved —- If on one side the tradition of Pischel (Rudrata's *Shringar Tilaka* and Ruyyak's *Sahradya Leela* 1886), Hermann Jacobi (Ruyyak's *Alankar Sarvaswa* 1908), Silva Levi (Indian Theatre 1890) to Sheldon Pollock (A Rasa Reader 2017) is visible, then on the other side Rajendralal Mitra (Agni Purana, Vishnudharmottara Purana 1873-78); People like Kashinath Pandurang Parab (Alankar Sarvaswa 1893; Vagbhattalankar 1895), Ramakrishna Kavi (Natyashastra 1926), Batuknath Sharma, Baldev Upadhyay (Natyashastra 1929), V. Raghavan (Shringar Prakash 1963), Kuppuswami Shastri (Pandurang Vaman Kane (Sahitya Darpan, History of Sanskrit Poetics 1923), Sushil Kumar Dey (History of Sanskrit Poetics 1923) to Manohar Kale, Bedekar, Ashok Ramchandra Kalekar, Reva Prasad Dwivedi, Rammurti Tripathi, Radhavallabha Tripathi were active; another tradition has been of scholars like Krishna Ryan who took the help of Sanskrit poetics to interpret contemporary Indian and Western work in English and in this process also tried to modernize Sanskrit poetics in the light of Western criticism. As a result, books like Suggestion and Statement in Poetry (1972), Text and Subtext (1887), The Burning Bush (1988), Sahitya: A Theory (1991) came out. With the concept of *dhwani*, not only the poems of Milton, Tennyson, T S Eliot, Yeats but also the novels of Thomas Hardy were discussed and with the help of Rasa Dhwani, an attempt was made to analyze the fiction of Nirmal Verma, Kiran Nagarkar, Loknath Bhattacharya, Rajendra Singh Bedi and the poems of Kumaran Aasan, Jayant Mahapatra, Dina Nath Nadeem, Nissim Ezekiel, P Lankesh and all. In this entire effort, as a critic has reminded us that we "must not forget that Alankar (figure of speech) is synonymous with poetic beauty. 'Rasa' is the name of the energy and fluidity contained in the composition, 'Riti' is the word composition (a well-formed combination of words) which follows the energy of the composition (energy is employed by the qualities prevalent in Rasa), 'Vakrokti' is the posture of expression (the initiating agent is talent) which makes poetic beauty possible and Dhwani (vyanjana vyapaar) is the targeted and untargeted process of reaching from word to meaning, which connects the statement with the context of life."[22] Is this a sign of the relevance of Sanskrit poetics?

Similarly, the Tolkappiyam, considered to be the oldest Tamil book, is often considered to be the original book of grammar, but a whole section of this book is focused primarily on poetics, which is considered to be the beginning of Tamil poetics. The Porultikaram section[23] of the book has nine chapters in which topics like types

22 Rammurti Tripathi, Ardhashati ka Bhartiya Kavya-chintan:vipaksha, aur pakshsa, Vani Prakashan, Delhi, 2000, p.36

23 An important study considering the third section of the Tolkappiyam suggested that the text was so revered because it was of special use to bards;

of poetry - Aham and Puram, poetic characteristics (Cheyulyil), poetic subjects - love episodes - secret love, marital love, stages and emotional state, figures of speech (similes), rhyme, sound (Iraichi), rasa (Meyappatiyal), poetic defects (Sutra 1591-92), tradition (Marpu), propriety (Munnam) and literary techniques etc. have been deliberated upon.[24] The first two chapters of the Porultikaram section are focused on Aham and Puram—these two categories have been created on the basis of subject matter, in which the poetry related to the inner world of a person (especially love life) is called Aham and the poetry making the outer world (social life, especially war) as their subject matter is called Puram. An attempt has been made in Tolkappiyam to view the inner and outer life, his conduct, by keeping it in the context of the natural environment and time and space; various moods and mental states of union and separation of man and woman have been envisioned by tying them in the cycle of nature and environment, flora and fauna, seasons and day and night.[25] On this basis, an attempt was made to analyze modern works, for example, on the basis of

---

it was a bardic grammar written for the training of young bards, which later became their indispensable handbook and canon. See K. Kailashpati, Tamil Heroic Poetry, Clarendon Press, Oxford, 1968, p. 49.

24 The entire account bears a strong resemblance to Bharata's Natyashastra, which is why one group of scholars considers it not only influenced by the Natyashastra but also translated from it, while another group speculates that the two texts—the Natyashastra and the Tolkappiyam—must have had a common lineage, which may have been lost over time. According to R. Nagaswamy the concept of Aham/Puram is derived from Bharata's Tandava/ Sukumar and the concept of Tinnai is derived from the Kakshaya Vibhaga. https://www.pgurus.com/dr-nagaswamy-reveals-how-tholkappiyam-follows-bharata-sastra-and-how-carnatic-music-got-its-name/accessed on 19/08/2022 and Ganesh Devy, Indian Literary Criticism, Orient Blackswan, Hyderabad, 2014

25 This entire discussion is based on classification like Sanskrit poetics, but unlike Sanskrit poetics. the focus of the analysis is centered on "content" and not on "form".

Tinnai, K. Ayyappa Panikkar analyzed Thakazhi Shivshankar Pillai's novel *Kayar* and V.J. Sebastian and Tamilavan tried to apply it for their practical criticism on some modern works. Similarly, such attempts were made in other South Indian languages as well, but soon the ineffectiveness of such attempts was exposed and such attempts started being seen as mere *interesting experiments*[26]. What was the reason for this? Why did this happen? Were the old concepts of Sanskrit or Tamil poetics incapable of understanding the new literature or was it a question of the inability or incapacity to apply the theoretical paradigm in practice or was there some other reason?

Noted Poet and thinker Jaishankar Prasad believed that, "The field in which the ideology of the critics of ancient Indian literature was working was somewhat different from the field of current criticism. In the knowledge-enhancing experience of this era, the widespread dominance of the western style of analysis on the hearts of Indians has started to be seen in action; but at the same time, in such analyses, the call for Indian-ness is also considered as a reaction, as a result; our ideology, due to mixed ideas, remains stuck in the quagmire of chaos."[27]

It is true that the parallel to visual and audible poetry, concepts of rasa and alankar were the product of historical time and sensibility, could still be useful for the fundamental analysis of beauty, but if it was proving inadequate for the interpretation and evaluation of any work, as one critic said that "Poetics does not explain poetry. There the critic itemizes examples according to

---

26 K.Sachidanandan, https://frontline.thehindu.com/columns/K_Satchidanandan/dilemmas-of-indian-literary-criticism/article5739887.ece

27 Vishnu Prabhakar, Rameshchandra Shah(eds) Prasad Rachna-Sanchayan, Sahitya Akademi, Delhi, 2010, p.415

his own formulations in a tailor-made manner — as a result, the natural progress of the —work- criticism - work, is not possible in which the meaning of the poem remains dynamic at many mixed levels."[28] So clearly this is a sign of poetics not being able to become practical criticism or of it being stagnant and as Namvar Singh has said that "To free criticism from stagnancy, there is a need to develop such a theory which is capable of analyzing the various expressions of ideology in literature, which begins with the scrutiny of language, then form and finally reveals the content. This task is not possible with the *received Rasa-Theory* or *available Dhwani Theory* or for that matter with any other school of Alankar Shastra."[29] Here, in the term *received Rasa-Theory* or *available Dhwani Theory*, there is an indication that it is not possible to accept it as it is, but if, while accepting it as tradition, in the modernist idiom, 'readiness to develop it and not blind imitation' is seen, then it is possible that what is said for the creative poet may also be applicable to the critic. Famous lines of T.S. Eliot's Tradition and Individual Talent are truly revealing: "Tradition is a matter of much wider significance. It cannot be inherited, and if you want it you must obtain it by great labour. It involves, in the first place, the historical sense, which we may call nearly indispensable to anyone who would continue to be a poet beyond his twenty-fifth year; and the historical sense involves a perception, not only of the pastness of the past, but of its presence; the historical sense compels a man to write not merely with his own generation in his bones, but with a feeling that the whole of the literature of Europe from Homer and within it the whole of the literature of his own country has a simultaneous existence and composes a simultaneous order.

---

28 Rammurti Tripathy.Ibid, p.32

29 Ibid, p.31

This historical sense, which is a sense of the timeless as well as of the temporal and of the timeless and of the temporal together, is what makes a writer traditional. And it is at the same time what makes a writer most acutely conscious of his place in time, of his contemporaneity."[30] The relevance of Indian poetics can also be determined by the fact that whether modern criticism in Indian languages has such *historical consciousness and knowledge of tradition* or not?

30 T.S.Eliot, Tradition and individual Talent in D.J.Enright, Ernst De Chickera (ed), English Critical Text, Oxford University Press, 2001, p.294

3

The Primal Text of Tamil Poetics: Porultikaram

If the world is the vocabulary of the poet, the conventions are his syntax.[31]

Tolkappiyam is often considered to be the first book of grammar, but a whole section of this book is focused on poetics, which can be considered the beginning of Tamil poetics. This great book is divided into three parts of which the Porultikaram section[32] has nine chapters containing deliberations on types of poetry—*Aham and Puram*, poetic characteristics (Cheyulyil), poetic subjects—love episodes—secret love, marital love, stages and emotional state of love, figures of speech (similes), meter, sound (Iraichi), rasa (Meyappatiyal), poetic defects (Sutra 1591-92), tradition (Marpu), propriety (Munnam) and literary techniques etc. And this entire description bears a lot of resemblance to Bharat's Natyashastra, which is why a group of scholars consider it not only influenced by

31 A.K.Ramanujan, The interior Landscape, New York Review Books, New York, 1967, Afterword

32 A critical study considering the third section of the Tolkappiyam suggested that the text was so esteemed because it was of particular use to bards. It was a bardic grammar written for the training of young bards, which later became their indispensable handbook and canon. See, K. Kailashpati, Tamil Heroic Poetry, Clarendon Press, Oxford, 1968, p. 49

Natyashastra but also a translated copy[33]. While the other group estimates that these two texts — Natyashastra and Tolkappiyam — must have had a common lineage, which is probably lost now[34]. Czech Indologist Kamil Václav Zvelebil (1927-2009) proclaims that Tolkappiyam in its current form, is a composition of the fifth century or later, which may not be the work of any individual but of a particular grammar-tradition[35]. Takanobu Takahashi's (1951--) study also shows that this work was not created in a day but it took six centuries to reach its current form; he demonstrated four layers of language in it and considered the oldest layer to be between the first and third century, while the second, third and fourth layers were estimated to be written between the fourth and sixth century.[36] It is also believed that the third section is the most recent. It is not surprising that most of the concepts of Natyashastra are compiled in this section. The method of analysis also matches the taxonomy of Sanskrit poetics.

The first two chapters of Porultikaram section are focused on Aham and Puram — both these categories have been created on the basis of subject matter, in which the poetry related to the inner world of a person (especially love life) is called Aham and the poetry taking the external world (social life, especially war)

---

33 According to R. Nagaswamy the concept of Aham/Puram is derived from Tandava/Sukumar of Bharata and the concept of Tinai is derived from Kakshaya Vibhaga, see, https://www.pgurus.com/dr-nagaswamy-reveals-how-tholkappiyam-follows-bharata-sastra-and-how-carnatic-music-got-its-name/accessed on 19/08/2022

34 G.N.Devy, Indian Literary Criticism, Orient Blackswan, Hyderabad, 2014

35 Kamil Václav Zvelebil, The Smile of Murugan, E.G.Bill, Leiden, Netherlands, 1973, p.146

36 Takanobu Takahashi, Tamil Love Poetry and Poetics, E.G. Brill, Leiden, New York, Conn., 1995, pp. 23-24

as its subject matter is called Puram. An attempt has been made to see the inner and external life of the person depicted in the poem, his behavior, in the context of the natural environment and his place and time in Tolkappiyam; various moods and mental states of union and separation of man and woman have been elaborated by tying them in the cycle of nature and environment, plants and animals, seasons and day and night. First sutra of the first chapter in section three States*: Kaikkilai mutlaap perunthinai iruvaya/murpataka kilanth elutinai amp*[37]*,* that means, there are seven stages of love starting from kaikkilai (unrequited, insatiable love) to perunthinai (illicit love) which are supposedly linked to the four regions in the next sutra: *avarul/nattuvan entinai nattuvanatu oliyap/pattuthirai vaayam paattiya panpe*[38]. That is, except for Palai (barren land) in the five Tinnai, these states of love occur only in the other four regions, namely Kurinchi (mountain), Neytal (sea-shore), Mullai (forest) and Marutham (river-bank), that is, complete unity of place and state of love is virtually possible. Then it was further associated with the environmental coordinates, that is, three dimensions of Aham poetry were considered: place-time (mutal), environment (karu) and state of love (Uri) and it was conceived in ascending order: *Mutal karu uripporul ainr moon/ nuvalum kaalai murai chirantanve/patalul payinrvai naatum kaalai*[39]. That means, according to the commentator, "In the sutra, the meaning of saying murai chirantatu i.e. "surpassing in ascending order" is that if the base (mutal) and the generated subject (*karu*)

---

37 Tolkappiyam, Dr. H. Balasubrahmanyam, Prof. K. Nachimuttu (Hindi translation), Central Institute of Classical Tamil, Chennai, First Edition, 2021, page 613

38 Ibid, p.615

39 Ibid, p.616

come in a poem, then *mutal* becomes the case of Tinnai (landscape, context) and if both come except *mutal*, then *karu* becomes the case for Tinnai. Whichever subject comes, the first described will become the subject, that is, Tinnai will be decided from that only.[40] In the next two sutras, it is also said that "People conversant with the characteristics and style say / it is not forbidden to mix Tinnai with each other / but there is no mixing of place." And "It is possible to be mixed / which is not uripporul i.e. not action."[41] That means, a mixture of *Mutal and Karu* is possible, but *Uri* means a mixture of love states is not possible. In the last sutra of the chapter, it is also instructed that the name of the hero and heroine should never be taken in a love affair, whereas in the poetry of Puram it is quite appropriate.

In the second chapter of Porultikaram section, Purattinayiyal, the concept of *Puram*, the opposite and complementary of the inner world described in the first chapter, has been presented — The concept of Aham/Puram includes many dualities like inner/ external; love/war; anacreontic/heroic; individual/social; private/ public . A.K. Ramanujan has written that while Aham poetry is a love poem, Puram is a poem based on all other subjects—goodness and badness, transitivity, community, empire— it is related to all; it is a public poem of ancient Tamil in which there is praise of the valor of kings, there are expressions of sorrow on the death of heroes, there is lamentation on the poverty of poets. Elegy, praise, condemnation, poems on tragic events and war are Puram poetry.[42] In *Kanchi* Tinai of Puram poetry, the sorrow caused by destruction and the futility of the world have also been depicted. But as George

40 Ibid, pp.616-617

41 Ibid, p.623

42 A, K, Ramanujan, ibid

L. Hurt proclaimed, the divisions and classification of Puram do not have any special meaning, the readers hardly get any assistance to understand or to appreciate the poetry.[43].

Aham and Puram, on one level, not only seem to be opposites but also complementary to each other. K. Kailashpati says that the early Tamil poetry (Sangam literature) is oral pastoral poetry[44] and this dichotomy of it — *Aham* and *Puram* is useful but when it comes to classifying a poem in one category or another, this concept seems cumbersome and artificial. Here it should also be remembered that the era reflected by this poem largely determines its subject matter and craft and that era was the era of valor and both categories of poems — Aham and Puram — were based on heroic characters. If the heroic tales focused on the physical strength of the hero, then the love poems showed the same character engaged in erotic activities; what is important here is that the society depicted by both categories of poems was an aristocratic society — a society of war heroes; whether they are mentioned by name or not. The world reflected in the poem was their world. There is ample evidence in both the poem and Tolkappiyam to establish the fact that the various activities of the aristocrats and elite classes were considered appropriate subjects for poetry[45].

---

43 George Luzern Hurt, Poets of the Tamil Anthology, Princeton University Press, Princeton, New Jersy, 1979, p.5

44 George Luzern Hurt has written that Kailashpati has tried to prove Sangam literature as oral poetry but he has failed because he has ignored the complex and sophisticated nature of Sangam literature." See, A History of Indian Literature, The Relation between Tamil and Classical Sanskrit Literature, Otto Harasowicz, Wiesbaden, Volume 10, Jane Gonda (Editor), 1976, page 327

45 K. Kailashpati, ibid, p.11

It has often been difficult to ascertain whether Tolkappiyam was composed on the basis of Sangam poetry or Sangam poetry was composed on the basis of Tolkappiyam, but Takanobu Takahashi has concluded on the basis of his research that Tolkappiyam was not a normative text and thirty-seven and a half percent of the works of Sangam literature disregard or reject the rules of Tolkappiyam[46]. It is true that in the creative process of a writer, the norms of criticism can be guiding but not complete regulators and moreover the parameters of criticism are formed from the process during comprehension of the work; the relationship between creation and criticism is never single but is dialectical. A.K. Ramanujan has rightly pointed out that the conventions of Sangam poetry do not seem to be the outcome of a work of rhetoric. The rhetorician summarized what was a live and continuing tradition. Because of the strength of this tradition some 500 poets appear to share to an unusual degree the poetic prescriptions of the Tolkappiyam.[47]

The next three chapters of the Porultikaram section - Kalviyal (secret love chapter), Karpiyal (marital love chapter), Poruliyal (remaining topics chapter) and the last chapter Marpiyal (tradition chapter) are also related to the content of literature, which again prove the centrality of content analysis in Tamil poetics. This is setting of a different kind of priorities in comparison to the form-centric Sanskrit poetics, but interestingly, in the analysis of the content, the famous *Natyadharmita* (Natak Valakkinum) of Bharata's Natyashastra has been accepted. Tolkappiyam had made it clear in a sutra of the initial chapter that what is the definition of poetry or

46 Takanobu Takahashi, ibid, p.225

47 A.K.Ramanujan, The interior Landscape, OUP, 1967, pp.100-101

how the descriptions of the behavior or conduct of the people takes the form of poetry. "The meeting of a man and a woman at a place, the emergence of affection between them, the occurrence of love between them called *Kalavu*, is a common practice. Scholars say that these events and behaviors are described in a lively and dramatic way as miracles and poetic creations, only then they take the form of poetry or literature.[48] Acharya Bharata in a sutra of the fourteenth chapter of Natyashastra, says: That is, when the actions of natural happiness and sorrows are performed with the help of body and other acts, then it should be considered as naatyadharmi[49]. And in a further sutra, he clearly declares: *Naatyadharmi pravrittam hi sada naatya prayojayet*[50]. That is, the dramatic experiment performed by the naatyadharmi should always be encouraged. In this chapter of Natyashastra, the *Kakshaya Vibhaga* has also been discussed which Dr. Nagaswamy considered as the basis of Tinnai.[51]

The remaining three chapters of Porultikaram, namely Meyappatiyal (Body-analysis-section), Uvamviyal (Upama-section) and Cheyulyil (Composition-section) — are very important as the book of poetics. Meyappatiyal (Body-analysis-section) has only twenty-six sutras in which ideas about the expression of emotions of the hero and heroine of the drama (Pannai) were discussed. Tolkappiyar says in the initial sutra itself that there are thirty-two emotions transmitted in the drama / if we think about it,

---

48 Tolkappiyam, ibid, pp.655-656

49 योऽयं स्वभावो लोकस्य सुखदु:खक्रियात्मक:।/सोऽङ्गाभिनयसंयुक्तो नाट्यधर्मी प्रकीर्तित:।14:79

50 नाट्यशास्त्रम, भाग 2, बाबूलाल शुक्ल शास्त्री(अनुवाद एवं व्याख्या), चौखम्बा संस्कृत संस्थान, वाराणसी, प्रथम संस्करण, 1978, पृष्ठ 198

51 See, https://www.youtube.com/watch?v=qpgQzoeZQhU (accessed on 21/08/2022)

only sixteen are visible outside.[52] Further, thirty-two emotions are mentioned, which are similar to the thirty-three *Vyabhichari Bhaavs* of Natyashastra. The first commentator of Tolkappiyam, Ilampurnar (11th century), has explained thirty-two by multiplying the eight *Sthayee Bhaavs* with four basic components. The reason, as it was commented upon, "To arrive at the number of sixteen, the *Hetu* and the resulting Sthayee Bhava were taken in a set called *Chuvai* (Rasa). The internal mental states and external physical conditions were taken in another set called Sattuvam (Satva). When these two are combined with the eight Meypādu (physical experience), the number of sixteen is obtained. In other words, the emotional object and its perception were taken as one unit. The experience of that emotion and its expression were taken in another unit."[53] This is the process of the emotion becoming Rasa. Bharata has mentioned in Natyasastra that, "The eight sentiments (rasa) recognized in drama are as follows: Erotic (sringar), Comic (hasya), Pathetic (Karuna), Furious (rudra), Heroic (vira), Terrible (bhyanaka), Odious (bhibhatsa), and Marvellous (adbhuta). The Dominant State (sthayibhava) are known to be the following: love, mirth, sorrow, anger, energy, terror, disgust and astonishment."[54] Abhinavgupta while explaining it in his *vivriti* (commentary) says that *Sringar* has been brought first because of its being available everywhere and easy to use and being known to all and pleasing to all. *Hasya* follows that *Sringar*. *Karuna* has been mentioned after it because it is an unbiased emotion. *Raudra* is the reason for *Karuna*

52 Tolkappiyam, ibid, p854

53 ibid, p865

54 Bharata-Muni, The Natyasastra, Tr, Manmohan Ghosh, Asiatic Society of Bengal, Calcutta, 1951 p.102 (रतिहसिश्च शोकश्च क्रोधोत्साहौ भय. तथा ।जुगुप्सा विस्मय्श्चेति स्थायिभावा: प्रकीर्तिता॥6:16-17 **श्रृंगार-हास्य**-करुण-रौद्र-वीर -भयानका:। वीभत्साद्भुतसंज्ञौ चेत्य्ष्टौ नाट्ये रसा:स्मृता:॥6:15 ॥)

and it is wealth oriented. *Veer* rasa has been kept after it because both *Kama* and *arth* (wealth) are based on religion and since it is based on religion and its purpose is to provide protection to the fearful, therefore *Bhayanak* has been mentioned after Veer rasa. Their *vibhaavs* (means for emotion) can be similar, therefore after that *Vibhatsa* rasa has been mentioned. In the end, only *Adbhuta* rasa should be placed.[55] In Tolkappiyam, where the sequence of emotions starts from *Nakai* (laughter) and reaches *Uvakai* (happiness) without any clear philosophical foundation, in Natyashastra, the journey of emotions from *Rati* (love) to *Vismaya* (wonder) has been linked to the familiarity of *purusharthas* and emotions; then, by dividing its causative *vibhaavs* into *aalambana* (basis) and *uddipana* (stimulant), a complex structure of emotions like *anubhava, Vyabhichari* (33) and *satvika* (8) has been created, which culminates in this famous rasa-sutra: *vibhavaanubhavavyabhicharisamyogyad rasanispatti:*[56]. Clearly, in the description of *Meyappatiyal,* only the body-experience is discussed.

The discussion on *alankar* as embellishment of the language is very old in India. According to the Rudradaman inscription, in the second century AD, it was considered essential to embellish with literary prose and poetry[57]. While discussing figures of speech for plays, Acharya Bharat has mentioned four alankaras — *Upama, Rupaka,*

---

55 Acharya Vishveshwar,(ed.) Hindi Abhinavbharti, Delhi University, Delhi, 2nd edition 1973, p.433

56 Ibid, p.442

57 P.V.Kane, History of Sanskrit Poetics, Motilal Banarasidas, Delhi, Reprint 2002, pp.372-73

Deepak, Yamaka[58] In which Upama was given the first place and while defining it, comparison was considered its core on the basis of similarity of quality and shape. Later *alankaarik* since Bhamaha[59], Dandi, Udbhata, Rudrata to Kuvalayanand, the number of four alankaras increased and reached up to one hundred and fifteen in number[60]. Whereas in Tolkappiyam only one alankar is described and that is simile, on which there is a whole chapter of thirty-seven sutras in Porultikaram. In the very first sutra Tolkappiyar says: Upama appears in four categories - action, result, form and colour. The commentator remarks: "While Tolkappiyar places Upama in four categories - action, result, form and colour, Dandi chooses only three areas of comparison - action, result and quality (panpu). Both form and colour come under panpu or quality."[61] Dandi[62], a South Indian Sanskrit poet and Acharya who lived in Kanchi in the 7th-8th century, presented the word Alankar in the general sense of the beautifier of poetry—- *Kavyashobhakaraan Dharmanalankaaran Prachakshate*. And made thirty-two sub-types of Upama. According to him, all alankaras can be divided into two types: *Swabhavokti* and *Vakrokti*. He called *Swabhavokti* as the primary or main figure of speech (Aadya Alankriti). By *Swabhavokti,* he meant the generic

58 उपमा रूपकंचैव दीपकं यमकं तथा ।काव्यस्यैते ह्यलङ्काराश्चत्वार: परिकीर्तिता: ॥ 17:43 ॥ The Natyasastra, ibid,

59 Bhamaha of the sixth century, while mentioning earlier famous five alankaras, divided the figures of speech in Kavyalankar into two kinds— Shabdalankar (2) and Arthalankar (36)— and described thirty-eight in number.P.V.Naganatha Sastry(ed), Kavyalankar of Bhamaha, Motilal Banarasidas, New, Delhi, Reprint1991, p.5

60 P.V.Kane, ibid, p.377

61 Tolkapiyyam, ibid, p.884

62 Anne e.Monius, The Many Lives of Dandin, International Journal of Hindu Studies, world heritage press, vol.4, april 2000

description of an object, or the general and direct description of an action, quality or substance[63]. Tolkappiyar, after making four types of Upama, made two sub-types of each, such as action and action indication, the outcome was divided into good result-giving and bad result-giving, form was divided into form and quantity. Colour was divided into colour-related and quality[64]. Tolkappiyam also emphasizes on naturalness. It is said in one sutra that "exaggeration or mitigation should be in accordance with the accepted norms". In the last sutra of this chapter, he also cautions against the excessive use of similes. It will be better to avoid/pile of similes. Excess of similes can decrease the beauty of poetry instead of increasing it. Therefore, it is necessary to use *Niral Nirattamittal* (in which many similes are used for one simile); *Nirlinrai* (in which simile and simile are decorated in a pair) and *Chunnam* (where simile and simile are used in a paired form) judiciously[65].

The composition section (Cheyulyil) of Porultikaram discusses various aspects of poetry or literary composition. This is the most detailed section of Porultikaram which contains two hundred and thirty-four *sutras*. First of all, thirty-four parts of poetry have been discussed — from syllable *(varna)* to *prabandha*, from the definition of poetry to meter and rhythm, from poetry types to genres, which are spread over and which have been divided into two unequal parts (26+8) and analyzed. According to the English translator of Tolkappiyam, S.V.Subramanian, the first twenty-six elements are general elements and the remaining eight are not only elements but

63 S.K.Dey, History of Sanskrit Poetics,

64 Tolkapiyyam, ibid, 896

65 Ibid, p. 909

are also considered genres of Tamil literature[66], whereas according to Dr. H. Balasubrahmanyam and Prof. Nachimuttu, the twenty-six elements of the first category apply to all types of poems, whereas the last eight elements are considered suitable for only *prabandha* poems by all critics[67]. Besides this, there is also a discussion about meaning (*kurippu moliye*), appropriateness (*munnam*) and the beauty that is created by the proper use of all the parts of the poem: *Beauty emerges in the poem from the proper use of the parts of the poem*[68].

In this chapter of the book, a very deep and valuable discussion has been done on the art of poetry. The detail in the discussion of the syllable, letter, vowel-consonant, meter, rhyme, rhythm can be gauged from the fact that thirteen thousand six hundred and ninety nine types of rhyme and alliteration (totai) alone have been mentioned. Four types of poetry have been discussed—*Achiriyam, Vanchi, Venpa* and *Kali* which make Dharma Artha Kama their subject matter. After its distinctions, seven types of literature (poetry)— Pattu (poetry), Ure (prose), Nul (classical text), Noti (riddle), Mutumoli (proverbs), Ankattam (satire), Pichi (riddles) have also been discussed. In this discussion, not only have they been defined, but an attempt has also been made to clarify all the characteristics of a particular genre with the help of their distinctions and sub-distinctions. Behind all these differences and sub-differences, Tolkappiyar has not allowed the synthesis in the concept of *Yaappu* to disappear, which is considered to be

66 S.V.Subrahamanium, Tolkapiyyam in English, Meiyappan Publishing House, Chidambaram, first edition 200 4, p 528

67 Tolkapiyyam, ibid, p.914

68 Ibid, p.1043

the essence of any work[69], he proudly declares in one place that, *Scholars say / Along with poetry, prose and knowledge-books / Mantra-Shastra, riddle, satire and proverb / creations in seven genres were in vogue / Various genres of literature are in the practice of the residents of the picturesque rich land / ruled by the kings of Chera, Chola, Pandya / surrounded by the mountain and sea from all four sides.*[70]

It is possible that all the genres of literature are in the practice of the residents of this picturesque rich land, but the work of discussing, analyzing and preserving it was definitely done by Tolkappiyam for which we must be grateful and obliged.

69 Ibid, p.957

70 Ibid

4

Panchatantra and Cervantes's Colloquium of Dogs

Panchatantra is one of the early texts of world literature in which anthromorphism was applied with great power. It challenged the anthropocentric belief that animals, plants and non-living things, unlike humans, lack spiritual and mental attributes. As a literary device, anthropomorphism is strongly associated with art and storytelling where it has ancient roots. Most cultures possess a long-standing fable tradition with anthropomorphized animals as characters that can stand as commonly recognized types of human behavior but as Max Muller had emphasized " Sanskrit literature is very rich in fables and stories; no other literature can vie with it in that respect; nay, it is extremely likely that fables, in particular animal fables, had their principal source in India . ...The best known of these collections of fables in Sanskrit is the Panchatantra, literally the Pentateuch, or pentamorone."[71] Panchatantra means Five Books or Systems. It is a collection of nearly ninety stories and stories within stories .The characters in these fables are animals as well as humans. The settings are situations of every day life in towns and villages, in palaces, on farms and in forests. The mood ranges from the didactic and cynical to the ribald and comic. The

---

71 F.Max Muller, On the Migration of Fables, http://books.google.co.in/books?id=fmMzDOQGZGwC&pg=PT65&lpg=PP1&dq=maxmuller+migration+of+fables

characters enact the foibles and follies, the virtues and the villainies of human conduct. They utter wise words and perform good deeds as well as indulge in every kind of sharp practice. Set in ancient India, they could exist at any time or place.[72]

No wonder Panchatantra became one of the pioneer texts in ancient world that was hugely successful in overcoming its linguistic and geographic boundaries. It was translated into Pahlavi in the sixth century and called *Kalila and Dimna*(after the two jackals that appear in the first chapter).An Arabic version was produced in the eighth century by the Persian writer Ibn al-Muqaffa; subsequently, it was also translates into verse. Persian versifications include a tenth-century version by Rudaki (of which only fragments remain), a version by Nasral-lah Abu al-Maali in 1144, and one by Hoseyn Vaiz Kashifi in the 16th century, *The Lights of Canopus*. In 1081, Simeon the son of Seph translated the Syriac version of *Kalila and Dimna* into Greek under the title *Stephanites kai Ichnelates* (The Crowned and the Tracker, an erroneous reading of the Arabic names Kalila and Dimna); subsequently, an Old Church Slavonic version was made from the Greek version. In the 13th century the Arabic version was translated into Spanish and Hebrew. Other translations followed: Latin (14th century), German (1470), and later French, English, and (in 1762) Russian. There are also translations into Turkish, Uzbek, Tatar, Malayan, and other Eastern languages.

To elevate the tastes of the Spanish common man, one of the literary works that Alfonso X (1221 – 1284) had chosen to be translated was *Kalila e Dimna .It is said that* this work had a huge

72 A.N.D.Haskar, Tales from the Panchatantra, National Book Trust, Delhi, Seventh Reprint, 2006, p.vii

popular impact in Spain especially its instructive intents. Examples can be cited from Historio del caballero de Dios que havia por nombre Cifar (Story of the knight of God called Cifar) (1299), Raimundo Lulio's the Libre de les maravilles (The Book of wonders) & Libere de les Besties (Book of Beasts), Don Juan Manuel's El Conde Lucanor (count Lucanor), Accipreste de Hita's Libro de Buen Amor, Clemente Sanchez Vercial's Libro de los exemplos (Book of examples) and so on.[73]

Cervantes (1547-1616), the famous author of *Don Quixote wrote* one dozen novellas exemplary just three years before his death in 1613.In the preface he writes:

I have called them 'exemplary', because if you rightly consider them, there is not one of them from which you may not draw some useful example; and were I not afraid of being too prolix, I might show you what savoury and wholesome fruit might be extracted from them, collectively and severally.

My intention has been to set up, in the midst of our community, a billiard-table, at which every one may amuse himself without hurt to body and soul; for innocent recreations do good rather than harm. One cannot be always at church, or always saying one's prayers, or always engaged in one's business, however important it may be; there are hours for recreation when the wearied mind should take repose. It is to this end that alleys of trees are planted to walk in, waters are conveyed from remote fountains, hills are leveled, and gardens are cultivated with such care. One thing I boldly declare: could I by any means suppose that these novels could excite any bad thought or desire in those who read them, I would rather cut off the hand with which I write them, than give

73 Enrique Gallud Jardiel, India in the Literature of Spain, B.R.Publishing Corporation, Delhi, 1992, p105.

them to the public. I am at an age when it does not become me to trifle with the life to come, for I am upwards of sixty-four.[74]

It is clear from this passage that author aims to achieve a role of an instructor or a moral teacher. English Translator of this text Walter K. Kelly rightly pointed out in the preface that

"It seems to be generally admitted that in rendering the title of a book from one language into another, the form of the original should be retained, even at the cost of some deviation from ordinary usage. Cicero's work _De Officiis_ is never spoken of as a treatise on Moral Duties, but as Cicero's Offices. Upon the same principle we have not entitled the following collection of tales, Instructive or Moral; though it is in this sense that the author applied to them the epithet exemplares_, as he states distinctly in his preface. The Spanish word 'exemplo', from the time of the archpriest of Hita and Don Juan Manuel, has had the meaning of 'instruction', or 'instructive story'."[75]

These instructive stories, it may be argued, like Panchatantra are structured in such a way that it contains stories within story or a series of incidences, illuminating each other with its contrasts and similarities. Characters are made prophetic through dialogue to reveal the moral of the story. Its illustrative character is fully matched with the mode of narration. One such example is "The colloquium of Dogs" that begins with the dialogue between two dogs namely, Scipio and Berganza; let's listen what they say:

---

74 Miguel De Cervantes Saavedra, Novellas Exemplars, (Tr.Walter K.Kelly), George Bell & Sons, London, 1881

http://www.gutenberg.org/catalog/world/readfile?fk_files=1495676 &page no=5

75 Ibid, p.2

"Scip._ Berganza, my friend, let us leave our watch over the hospital to -night, and retire to this lonely place and these mats, where, without being noticed, we may enjoy that unexampled favour which heaven has bestowed on us both at the same moment.

Berg._ Brother Scipio, I hear you speak, and know that I am speaking to you; yet cannot I believe, so much does it seem to me to pass the bounds of nature.

Scip._ that is true, Berganza; and what makes the miracle greater is that we not only speak but hold intelligent discourse, as though we had Souls capable of reason; whereas we are so far from having it, that the difference between brutes and man consists in this, that man is a rational animal and the brute is irrational.

"Scip._ Let us proceed in this manner, friend Berganza: to-night you shall relate the history of your life to me, and the perils through which you have passed to the present hour; and to-morrow night, if we still have speech, I will recount mine to you; for it will be better to spend the time in narrating our own lives than in trying to know those of others."[76]

Then Berganza goes on narrating episodes after episodes of his life — from slaughter-house to fellow Alguazil & attorney to the street showman drummer to the lady magician Canizares to the world of Gypsies to a Christian fellow of Moorish descent to a drama company with poet & comedian and finally reaching to Mahudes hospital .In this journey the main focus is on human nature with all its ironies and contradictions. Story unfolds in such a way that its conclusion turns into a kind of moral aphorism that can be easily

---

76 Ibid, pp.94-95

comparable to the narrative structure of Panchatantra, for example see the following aphorisms:

Be wary with your tongue, for from that member flow the greatest ills of human life.[77]

Ill-doing is so easily learned, since it comes by a natural obliquity.[78]

Wisdom in a poor man lies under a cloud, and cannot be seen; or if by chance it shines through it, people mistake it for folly, and treat it with contempt.[79]

Humility is the base and foundation of all virtues, and that without it there are none. It smoothers inconveniences, overcomes difficulties, and is a means which always conducts us to glorious ends; it makes friends of enemies, tempers the wrath of the choleric, and abates the arrogance of the proud: it is the mother of modesty, and sister of temperance. [80]

Similar examples can be cited here from Panchatantra for comparative study but more pertinent is the fact to underline here is that when scipion keeps reflecting and commenting upon the various life episodes of Berganza one after another, it turns into a series of mirror where images of human life with all its nakedness can be visualized. The uniqueness of Cervantes's narrative art lies in the fact and what makes it contemporary and quite different from Panchatantra is its ability to throws light to the object at the same time revealing the very source and nature of the light. It never let the reader forget that he or she is reading a fictional work.

---

77 Ibid, p.97.

78 ibid, p.

79 ibid, p.128

80 ibid, p.101

See what Scipion advices to Berganza: "some stories are pleasing in themselves, and others from the manner in which they are told; I mean that there are some which give satisfaction, though they are told without preambles and verbal adornments; while others require to be decked in that way and set off by expressive play of features, hands, and voice; whereby, instead of flat and insipid, they become pointed and agreeable. Do not forget this hint, but profit by it in what you are about to say."[81] In some place he suggests how not to write satires, as it is a difficult art: "I have heard that it was a saying of a great poet among the ancients, that it was a difficult thing to write satires. I consent that you put some point into your remarks, but not to the drawing of blood. You may hit lightly, but not wound or kill; for sarcasm, though it make many laugh, is not good if it mortally wounds one; and if you can please without it, I shall think you more discreet." [82] In some other place he points out how philosophy is bad for writing: "Beware, Berganza, that this inclination to philosophize is not a temptation of the fiend; for slander has no better cloak to conceal its malice than the pretence that all it utters are maxims of philosophers, that evil speaking is moral reproval, and the exposure of the faults of others is nothing but honest zeal. There is no sarcastic person whose life, if you scrutinize it closely, will not be found full of vices and improprieties. And now, after this warning, philosophize as much as you have a mind."[83]

This is self-conscious art — a kind of metafiction, as it is commonly believed that "metafictional novels tend to be constructed

81 ibid, p.97

82 ibid, p.98

83 ibid, p.104

on the principle of a fundamental and sustained opposition: the construction of a fictional illusion (as in traditional realism) and the laying bare of that illusion. In other words, the lowest common denominator of metafiction is simultaneously to create a fiction and to make a statement about the creation of that fiction .The two processes are held together in a formal tension which breaks down the distinctions between 'creation' and 'criticism' and merges them into the concepts of 'interpretation' and 'deconstruction'. "[84]

'The colloquium of Dogs' is a creation and criticism both at the same time as story ends with a revelation: "The licentiate finished the reading of this dialogue, and the Alferez his nap, both at the same time. "Although this colloquy is manifestly Fictitious," said the licentiate, "it is, in my opinion, so well composed, that the Señor Alferez may well proceed with the second part."

"Since you give me such encouragement, I will do so," replied the Alferez, "without further discussing the question with you, whether the dogs spoke or not." [85]

It is a magic moment not because when senor Alferez was making these dogs speak during his nap, licentiate was reading this dialogue instantly in his waking state but in a unique way it 'interprets' and 'deconstructs' this very story and our lives too! We all feel like dogs who got only one night to speak out our life-sufferings and that too in sleep when we wake up it turn out to be 'manifestly fictitious' !!!

---

84 Patricia Waugh, Metafiction: The Theory and practice of self-conscious Fiction, Methuen & co.USA, First Published 1984, p.5

85 Miguel De Cervantes Saavedra, ibid, p.128

5

Muslim Women Voice of Bhakti in Pre-Modern North-India

It was not common to be a Muslim woman and a Hindu devotee, especially in the 17th century of north India but this is exactly the case with Taj Bibi (c.b.1643) and Sekh Rangrezin (c.1655). Though we have no historical account about their life, but legends and hagiographical writings regarding them unequivocally emphasize their initial Muslim identity, submerging into all powerful emotion called *Bhakti*[86] (devotion) later. And if we take their poetry into consideration, this narrative becomes more corroborative and sometimes more conclusive.

The hagiographical writings in Pushtimarg categorically indicate Taj as contemporary of Akbar (1542-1605) and Gosain Vitthalnath (1516-1588) but literary historians put her usually in

86 *As John Carmanhas pointed out, the term bhakti is used specifically to describe the human response to God and never to characterize God's response to human beings. In actively encouraging participation (which is a root meaning of bhakti), the poets represent bhakti as a theology of embodiment. Their thesis is that engagement with (or participation in) God should inform all of one's activities in worldly life. The poets encourage a diversity of activities, not limiting bhakti to established modes of worship—indeed, some poets harshly criticize such modes—but, instead, making it the foundation of human life and activity in the world. As a theology of embodiment, Bhakti is embedded in the details of human life.* The Embodiment of Bhakti, Karen Pechilis Prentiss, Oxford University Press, New York Oxford 1999, p.8

seventeenth century. Taj got her first mention in the Hindi literary historiography *Shivsingh Saroj* (1877) where her birth year is ascribed to 1595 A.D[87] but according to Kishorilal Gupt, it's not her birth year but writing period.[88] Later in *Mahila Mriduvani* (1905) edited by Devi Prasad Munshif (1848-1923) speculated her birth year 1643 A.D., and *Mishrabandhu Vinod* (1913) describes her as a major poet of Senapati-Period (1624-1649).[89]Later her presence in seventeenth century was generally accepted as it was testified in one of her poems where she recounts poets of yore like Sur, Tulsi, Raidas, Nanak, Malook, Dhanna, Namdeo, Dadu, Kabir, Meera—and all of them are pre-seventeenth century:

I've *seen the savior of Dhruv, Prahlad, Gaj and Graha/ To Ahilya to jackals and vultures to vibhisan/.Whether it is Sinner Azamil or Sur, Tulsi, Raidas/Nanak, Malook or Taj everyone is loved by Hari. / Whether it is Dhani, Namdev, Dadoo or butcher Sadna/Courtesan, Kabir or Meera everyone is endeared by Hari/I heard his name in the world's affair everywhere/I know the Vallabh of Radha, Krishna -Vallabh is mine*[90]

---

87 this book was based on some anthologies of earlier centuries like *Kalidas Hazara* in which one thousand composition of 212 poets(including Taj & Sekh) between the period of 1423 to 1718 A.D. was compiled according to its compiler Kalidas Trivedi, see, Saroj Sarvekchan, Kishorilal Gupta, Hindustani Akademi, Allahabad, first edition 1967, pp.65-66

88 see, ibid, p.335

89 Mishrabandhu Vinod, part I, Ganga Pustak Mala Karlaya, Lucknow, 2nd Edition, 1927, p110

90 ध्रुव से प्रहलाद गज ग्राह से अहिल्या देखि /स्योरी और गीध यौ विभीषण जिन तारे हैं ./पापी अजामिल सूर तुलसी रैदास कहूं /नानक मलूक 'ताज' हरि ही के प्यारे हैं /धनी नामदेव दादू सदना कसाई जानि, /गनिका कबीर मीरा सैन उर धारे हैं। /जगत को जीवन जहां बीच नाम सुन्यो /राधा के वल्लभ कृष्णा वल्लभ हमारे हैं ॥ Hindi ke Musalmaan Kavi, Ganga Prasad Singh,'Visharad'(ed.), Lahri Book Depot, Kashi, 1926, p.163

In this poem what is also remarkable is putting herself along with other poets of repute in the company of mythological characters and the proportion is equal——ten mythological with ten historical — but is it intentional? What could be the motive of this proposed interaction of the two? The cultural historian Rajeswari Sunder Rajan views the idea of representation as just such an intersection between private and public, reality and culture, and the real and the imagined: "The concept of 'representation', it seems, is useful precisely because and to the extent that it can serve a mediating function between the two positions, neither foundationalist (privileging 'reality') nor superstructural (privileging 'culture'), not denying the category of the real, or essentializing it as some pre-given metaphysical ground for representation.[91]

There are two sets of legend regarding Taj Bibi, the famed and most talented poetess of medieval North- India after Meera Bai[92] —-one is prevalent among pushtimargi circle, where she is wife of Akbar (1542-1605), the great Mughal monarch and other legend mainly reported by Govind Gilla Bhai (1848-1926), a Brajbhasha poet from Bhavnagar, Gujarat. He has reported to Jyoti Prasad Mishra 'Nirmal', (famed editor of *Stree Kavita kaumodi*) in a letter dated 11.12.1925 that, " There was A Muslim woman named Taj in Karauli village, who was very particular to visit temple for *darshan* every day after having bath and then only she used to have her food. One day, she was not permitted for *darshan* by the Vaishnavas as she was considered heretic. So she didn't leave the temple premise that day and kept murmuring Krishna's name all along. Thakur ji

---

91 The Embodiment of Bhakti, Karen Pechilis Prentiss, Oxford University Press, New York Oxford 1999, p.8

92 see, Madhyakalin Hindi Kaviyatriyan, Savitri Sinha, Aatmaram and sons, Delhi, First Edition 1953, p.193

himself appeared in front of her with food plate in his hand, saying, "you didn't have *prasad* a bit today, now take it..." when in the morning Vaishnavas arrived there, she narrated the whole story to them...all of them have fallen to her feet. And then after Taj started receiving *prasad* after *darshan* every day. So thereafter it became customary that Taj enters first for the darshan of Thakurji and then other Vaishnavas will follow.

"All this I heard from so many Vaishnavas when I visited Karauli.I have listened so many poems of her too...I had copied so many of it too. I have two hundred poems of Taj in my personal library in my own hand- writing."[93]

Another set of legends belongs to Vaisnava hagiography, especially 'Bhavsindhu' and 'Sri Govardhan ji ke prakatya' has particular reference to the legend of Taj. There is a portion in 'Bhavsindhu' called *Taj Bibi ki Varta*[94], where she is portrayed as one of the wives of Emperor Akbar. One day, as story goes Akbar got made one painting of Gosain Vitthalnath (1516-1588) by his painter after meeting with this inspiring son of legendary Vallabhacharya (1479-1531) in Mathura and installed it in his palace.[95]Now it became his daily chore to look first at that painting with absolute reverence before doing anything after getting up in the morning. Later Taj shifted this painting to her chamber, so Akbar has to come there every day. Consequently Taj became very devout to Gosain ji Her two close friends, daughter of Birbal Shobhavati and Rai Vrindavan Das's daughter were devotee of

93 Quoted in Stree Kavita Kaumodi, Jyoti Prasad Mishra 'Nirmal'(ed).Gandhi Hindi Pustak Bhandar, Prayag, 1931 p.21

94 Bhav-Sindhu, Swami Gokulnath, Publisher:Lallu Bhai Chhagan Lal Desai, Amadabad, second edition 1936, pp.297-312

95 Bhav Sindhu, ibid, pp.291-296

Gosain Vitthalnath. Taj used to be very afraid of the fact that Akbar may neglect her under the spell of his other wives. So one day she sent Shobhavati to Gosain ji for asking remedy for this —how to keep husband under control. Gosain ji has composed one couplet and given it to Shobhavati saying that Taj should wear it in her neck after framing it in gold. When this news reached to those queens, they traduced Akbar that Taj has spelled black magic on him, and its *mantra* she wears in an amulet all the time on her neck. Queens expressed their apprehension and anxiety about the probable mishap of the king. Akbar enquired about it and found truth in it —the golden locket was hanging on her neck; when it was opened one piece of paper was found there on which this couplet was written there: *Wishes, philters, amulets, clean them all/Do what your loved one says, automatically he will be yours all*[96] When Akbar came to know that this couplet was sent by Gosain Vitthalnath, he said Taj to ask him anything she wishes. Taj shown rather her eagerness for initiation from Gosain Ji and that was granted by the emperor. After initiation, it seems she became totally devoted to Lord Krishna as she declares daringly in one of her poems:

Listen dear, my heart's story/I'm sold to you shall too tolerate ignominy/Forgetting words of Quran or being a Muslim/Shall internalize all your attributes, determined to worship idol,/Dedicated to your crown of dark charming head/Shall remain unblemished in the blemish of your love./O son of Nand, I am lost to you/Shall be with you dear as devout hinduwani for you.[97]

---

96 कामन, टामन, टोटका, ये सब डारौ धोय |
पिया कहै सो कीजिए, आपहिं ते बस होय || ibid, p.297

97 सुनो दिल जानी मेरे दिल की कहानी /तुम दस्त ही बिकानी बदनामी भी सहूँगी मै।/देव पूजा ठानी मै निवाज हूँ भुलानी /तजे कलमा कुरआन साड़े गुनन गहूँगी मै/।स्यामला सलोना सिर ताज सिर कुल्ले दिए/तेरे नेह दाग में निदाग हो दहूँगी मैं ॥/नन्द के कुमार कुर्बान तोडी सूरत पे/ताड़ नाल प्यारे हिन्दुआनी हो रहूँगी मै ॥ Mahila Mriduvani, *Deviprasad 'Munshif'(ed), p.34*

This particular poem is very popular not only in Pushtimargi circles[98] but to some extant in popular music[99] in India till today.

There are also few tales about the last days of Taj in true hagiographical tradition. In one of the stories, it is narrated that in her last days she felt deep within her heart a kind of great separation (mahaviraha) from her lord. In one of the poems, it seems she portrayed her condition of that time in this way: *My love resides on mountain and me on the banks of Yamuna/now meeting is really tough, since my feet are chained/if I stay at Agra, and my lord resides on mountain/by breaking my chain with force, Certainly I shall be with my love.*[100]

Realizing her grave condition Akbar himself took her to Govardhan[101]—the moment they reach, as story goes they found Kumbhandas and Govind Swami(?) were singing a certain Dhamar, a Taj's composition. She became utter restless and uncontrollable in love. Daughters of Rai Vrindavandas and Birbal tried her to hold

---

98 See, Suno Dil Jaani Bhajan Under Bhaktmal Katha Of Taaj Begam By Pujya Sant Sh. karun Dass Ji Maharaj (https://www.youtube.com/watch?v=0-DEILfO3iM) also see, Taaj Begum Ka Likha Hua Bhaw Krishna Ji Ke Liye, krishna swami ji maharaja, (https://www.youtube.com/watch?v=bKzmYHfCWmo)

99 Song : Suno Dil Jaani, Album : Piya Ke Rang Rang Deeni , Singers / Music : J. S. R. Madhukar *(https://www.youtube.com/watch?v=4 ZZvy2VFaKg)*

100 प्रीतम बसत पहाड़ पे हम यमुना के तीर ।अबको मिलनो कठिन है पाँवन पडी जंजीर ॥

अगर आगरो मो रह्यो गिरि पर बसे मो नाथ ।तोरी जंजीर जोम सों और मै प्रीतम के पास ॥ Bhav Sindhu, ibid, p305

101 See, the conclusion of J.S.Hawley;"In many narratives of the period we have been reviewing, Akbar emerges less as a Muslim than as a ruler, patron, classifier, and paradigmatic aesthete." John Stratton Hawley, Three Bhakti Voices,(Mirabai, Surdas, and Kabir in their Time and Ours), Oxford University Press 2005, p.193

her but only could find her physical dead body since her spiritual self merged into *leela*. Akbar remarked that thing reached where it belonged to. [102]

There is a slightly different version of this episode in Goswami Harirai's *Shreenath Ji Ki Prakatya Varta* where lord Shreenath ji(Lord Krishna, aged seven) plays chess in Agra with Taj, (daughter of Ali Khan Pathan and wife of Emperor Akbar) so knowing this; chess was also introduced in the temple by the order of Sri Gosain ji. One day when emperor with all his begums camped in shree Giriraj ji's place, Taj went for Shreeji's *darshan* where seeing him in person she left her physical body, merging her spiritual self into His being. Everyone was shocked to see this and consequently became very afraid of facing Akbar but by the grace of Shreenath ji he only remarked that *don't worry, thing has reached where it belonged.*[103]

Another legend that is also very often circulated in the Pushtimargi circles regarding Taj is that Sri Nathji used to visit her every night and play Chaupad and chess with her till late at night. At one instance when Sri Vithal Nathji opened the portals of the Mandir at Mangala Darshan he found Sri Nathji lying in a Suthan and Pataka which is a Muslim dress which he had never created for the Swarupa. So he asked. Sri Nathji told: "This is gifted to me by Taj Bibi and I like this dress". From that day as the legend goes that Sri Thakurji began to wear a jari Suthan and Patka.

Historically speaking it's difficult to pin point life-narrative of Taj in any assured manner as legends, unlike history do not follow exact chronology. Taj is also identified with the famous

---

102 Bhav Sindhu, ibid

103 Shreenath ji ki Prakatya varta, Goswami Harirai, Vidya Vibhag, Shreenathdwara, 1919, p.41

Mumtaz Mahal, wife of Shah Jahan (1592 – 1666), who under the pen name of Taj' used to write poetry.[104] As far as birth place of Taj is concerned there are three places—-Karauli (Rajasthan), Punjab and Eastern India that are asserting their claim. Karauli was described by Govind Gilla Bhai as he himself happened to gather this information from Vaishnavas in Karauli itself. Swami Gokulnath (1551-1640) has mentioned Taj as Punjabi in his book *Bhavsindhu*[105]and the presence of few Punjabi words in her poems *really* substantiate this claim as Mishrabandhu too emphasized this fact.[106] Ganga Prasad Singh 'Visharad' in his anthology *Hindi ke Musalmaan Kavi* (Muslim Poets of Hindi) (1926) quoted one couplet of Taj and proved that she was born in eastern India. The quoted poem was as follows: पूरब ले जनम कमाई जिन खूब करी/पाय तन दीन 'ताज' सुनी बेद बानी है means Born in east to earn a lot /got a humble body to listen the voices of Veda[107]but here, the word पूरब ले जनम is problematic as Kishorilal Gupta has rightly pointed out that it पूरब ले are not two distinct words but right word is पूरबले one word and it really makes more sense if we read it as पूरबले जनम (previous birth) rather than पूरब ले जनम (born in east)[108]

Similarly the legend of Shekh is equally bleary. According to popular legends, Shekh was a Rangrejan (dyer) and one day when she was about to dye certain turban she found there is a knot in which a piece of paper is tied in it —out of curiosity she untied the knot and found that something is written on the paper —-she read

104 Stree Kavita Kaumodi, ibid

105 Bhavsindhu, ibid, p.309

106 Mishrabandhu Vinod, Part ii, Ganga Pustak Mala Karlaya, Lucknow, 2nd Edition, 1927, p.417;Savitri Sinha too mentions that she was residents of Punjab, see, Madhyakalin Hindi Kaviyatriyan, ibid, p 192

107 Hindi ke Musalmaan Kavi, ibid, p.164

108 Saroj Sarvekchan, ibid, p.335

it: *Why golden stick like damsel has so little waist*[109]; she thought it was the poetry in the nature of problem-solving (समस्या-पूर्ति) so she solved it by composing this supplementary line: *Since by cutting gold from the waist nature had kept it on the breast*[110]. And after dying the turban she tied the knot exactly on the same place with that paper adding her lines in it. When the customer, who happened to be a budding Brahmin poet got his dyed turban he found that there is a knot in it, he opened it and found surprisingly that his incomplete lines got perfect match—he rushed to the dyer enquiring about its author and when he came to know he simply proposed her and immediately converted to Islam to marry her.[111] Thereafter they

---

109 कनक छरी-सी कामिनी काहे ते कटि छीन, Hindi Sahitya ka Aadha Itihash, Suman Raje, Bhartiya Gyanpith, Delhi, Third Edition 2006, quoted on p.156

110 कटि को कंचन काटि विधि कुचन मध्य धरि दीन, ibid

111 Munshif Devi Prasad has mentioned this composition in this context:" प्रेम रंग पगे जगमगे जगे जामिनी के /जोबन की जोति जगि जोर उमगत हैं /मदन के माते मतवारे ऐसे घूमत हैं /झूमत हैं झुकि झुकिझंपि उघरत हैं /आलम सा नवल निकाई इन नैननि की /पांखुरी पदुम पे भंवर थिरकत हैं and shekh has completed it in this way:चाहत हैं उडिबे कौ देखत मयंक-मुख /जानत है रैनि ताते ताहि में रहत हैं ।।. (This piece was translated into English long back in 1923 by Mrs. Keay as follows: Alam Speaks: The bright eyes of a beautiful woman,/awake all night long, are full of love/It seems, as one looks at her, that youth is flowing from her/ Those eyes are moving towards intoxicated with love/They are cast down, being heavy with sleep and sometimes they are wide open/O Alam, some new beauty is seen in these eyes/They appear like a bee hovering over a lotus flower./Shekh Rangrezin Replies: Those eyes that are like a bee want to fly away /when the behold the face of the moon/But knowing that it is night, they remain in the lotus flower."Poems by Indian Women, Margaret Macnicol, Oxford University Press, 1923, p.75)

Pandit Nakchedi Tiwari has mentioned another kavitts in this context:घूंघट जमानिका है कारे कारे केश निशि ;/खुटिला जराय जरे दीपक उजारी है /बाजत मधुर मृदुवाणी सो मृदंग धुनि नैना नट नागर लकुट लटधारी है /आलम सुकवि कहै रति विपरीत समै श्रम विन्दु अंजुली पहुप भरि डारी है .अधर सुरंग भूमि नृपति अनंग आगे नृत्य करे बेसर की मोती नृत्य कारी है ।।" Hindi ke Musalmaan Kavi, ibid, quoted on p.113

lived happily with joint venture of poetry writing all their life. They were also blessed with one son named Jahan and there is also one legend associated with him. Once prince Muazzam asked shekh jokingly, "Are you wife of Aalam? Shekh replied instantly. "Yes my lord (jahanpanah), I am, of course, mother of Jahan."[112] This particular legend marks a great sense of humour and attitude unusual for a writer especially for a women writer in medieval times.

Shekh Rangrejan was first mentioned in the literary historiography of Shivsingh Saroj (1877) where her period of writing is given 1583 to 1623 A.D. and also mentioned that her kavitts were compiled in *Kalidas Hazara,* an anthology of repute compiled in 1718 A.D.[113] Quoting one particular poem of Aalam he tried to prove that he was contemporary of prince Muazzam Shah (1643- 1712) son of Mughal emperor Aurangzeb (1618 –1707) but later critic pointed out that word *Aalam* used in above quoted poem simply means world and it is not *chhap* of the poet and moreover this particular poem is not to be found in any other collection of the poet.[114] When the manuscript of *Aalam-keli,* the joint poetic venture of Aalam and shekh was discovered in 1903 A.D. in Saraswati Bhandar of Maharaja of Banaras, Samvat 1753(1696 A.D) is mentioned as the date of writing(lipikal) in it. Taking clues from all these facts, Lala Bhagwan Din while editing for its publication in 1922 established their working period (rachana kal) between

---

112 Quoted in Lala Bhagvandin(ed.), Aalam-Keli, Publisher:Umashankar Mehta, Ram Ghat, Kashi, 1922, p.5

113 Shivsingh Saroj.ibid, p.806

114 Vishwanath Prasad Mishra, Hindi Sahitya ka Atit, Vani Prakashan, Delhi, 2014, pp.297-308

1683-1723A.D.)[115]He also speculated that Shekh must be residents of Punjab as it is evident from the forms of pronoun and verb used by her in the poetry.[116]Although critic like Parshuram Chaturvedi considers their residency somewhere in Jaunpur district, but provides no proof for this conclusion[117].

The question is how to read the life-narratives of Taj and Sekh depicted in legends and hagiography? If we take Grimm brothers' definition of legend as a folktale historically grounded[118]Are these folk legends of our medieval poetess more poetic than historical in the sense Norbert Krapf has articulated it in his study? He writes, *"The fairytale is more poetic, the legend is more historical; the former exists in its innate blossoming and commotion, the legend, by contrast, is characterized by a lesser variety of colours, yet it represents something special in that it adheres always to that which we are conscious of and know well, such as a locale or a name that has been secured*

---

115 Lala Bhagwan Din,(ed.) Aalam Keli, Umashankar Mehta Publication, Ramghat, Kashi, 1922, p.3

116 Ibid, p6

117 Aalam Granthāvalī, Vidyanivas Mishra(ed), Vani Prakashan, Delhi, 2000, p.iii

118 *The definition includes three main factors: I. the legend fits within the narrator's concept of historical time; a. the legend is connected with a definite historical (real or fabulous) event, b. the legend is connected with a definite person, that is, a named historical (real or fabulous) figure; 2. the legend fits the narrator's concept of geographical space, that is, it is connected with a definite place; 3. the legend is a true story; although it deals with supernatural events, it is "believed" by its bearers, and it is regarded as pertaining to the real world of the narrator and his audience (the fairy tale, to the contrary, is not believed by the narrating community, although it too deals with supernatural events)* Concerning the "Historical" and the "Local" Legends and Their Relatives, Heda Jason, The Journal of American Folklore, Vol. 84, No. 331, Toward New Perspectives in Folklore (Jan. - Mar., 1971), p.134

through history. Because of this local confinement, it follows that legend cannot, like the fairy tale finds its home anywhere."[119] Historically speaking seventeenth-century India is less turbulent and more settled as far as political stability, economic prosperity or religious activity is concerned. Historian has rightly pointed out that, "At the beginning of the seventeenth century, the liberal attitudes toward religion set in place by Akbar predominated in much of north India, but as the century advanced a sense of conservatism set in. Hand in hand with these new attitudes and increased wealth, rulers from all areas in India increasingly built elaborate and often large temples, mosques and shrines, to proclaim their own particular religious affiliations."[120] In the literary field bhakti (devotion) and sringar (erotic) were the two main pre occupations for poetic engagements and their form and nature was determined by the fact that whether that was going to be performed in the court or in the temple, imaginary or real. In the case of Taj both legend and poetry reveals her fascination for bhakti, whereas poetry of Sekh does emphasize her devotion towards lord Krishna but legends are silent about it—— she is not perceived as saintly as Taj.

The Hindi world of the seventeenth century is mainly mannerist (riti pradhan) but most of the poetry of Taj and Sekh testifies their personal style of expression. They didn't write in 'Pad style', much familiar and tested meter for Krishna-themes but chosen Kavitt-sawaiyya meter.[121] They also, like other poets of their time, never

---

119 Beneath the Cherry Sapling: Legends from Franconia, edited & Translated Norbert Krapf, Fordham University, 1988, p.7

120 India before Europe, Catherine B. Asher and Cynthia Talbot, Cambridge University Press, First South Asian Edition 2008 p.186

121 *Savitri Sinha expressed her surprise to note the faultless style and rhythm of meter in Taj as that time mostly queens were writing Krishna poetry and for them the knowledge of prosody was not impossible but to achieve such a height for a common person like Taj, it is exceptional. Madhyakalin Hindi Kaviyatriyan Ibid, p190*

forget to emphasize the agency of poet by putting their name (chhap) in the poems, either in first person or in the third person. This poem of Sekh, for example; *Friends, since the time Gopal has shifted to Madhuvan/our Madhuvan turned hostile like a devil/Sekh says, birds of Kadamb tree on the banks of Kalindi — parrots, Peacocks, Starlings, wagtails, troubling me /and this black cuckoo just wants to scrape my heart away/whom to blame when cuckoo becomes crow to squabble with me.*[122]or see how Taj describes about Lord Krishna and claims her propriety on Him: *He is gallant and smug, colorific with all colours/Very resolute, so different from other deity. /Garland adores the neck, white pearl the nose/Earring enchants with red crown on his head./Kills all malicious but rescues every sage or hermit,/'Taj', who beholds your mind, truly loves thine./Darling of Nand who knocked down Kansa/Frolic of Vrindavan Krishna Sahib is mine.*[123]

Unlike Taj, Sekh does not believe in imagery, most of the times she describes her emotions as after-thought impressions in straight forward manner without any frills. Like other poets of her time, she hardly show any inclination towards artificial ornamentation or formal poetic craft rather her poetry shows affiliation towards simple authentic voice of a true Bhakta, like: *Straight is the footstep but doors arduous/Devotion is robust where no guards around./'Sekh', There lives my king of three worlds/He is the king of Gods, helping poors around./For enemy, neither animosity nor coercion/No prohibition but all powers for those unsound./The honks of elephant may reach*

---

122 जब ते गुपाल मधुवन को सिधारे माई/मधुवन भयो मधु दानव विषम सों।'सेख' कहै सारिका सिखंडी खंडरीच सुक/मिली के कलेस कीन्हौ कालिंदी कदम सों।देह करि करठा करेजो लीन्हों चाहति है/काग भई कोईल कगाई करे हम सों। Hindi ke Musalmaan Kavi, ibid, quoted on p.119

123 छैल जो छबीला, सब रंग में रंगीला, बड़ा चित्त का अड़ीला, कहूं देवतों से न्यारा है। माल गले सोहै, नाक-मोती सेत सोहै, कान कुंडल मन मौहे, मुकुट सिर धारा है।। दुष्ट जन मारे, संतजन रखवारे, 'ताज' चित्त में निहारे, प्रेम प्रीति करन वारा है। नन्दजू का प्यारा, जिन कंस को पछारा, वह वृन्दावनवारा, कृष्ण साहेब हमारा है।। ibid, p.163

bit late /But Ant's scream reaches time -bound.[124] Simplicity, not the mediocrity is the high point of Bhakti poetry since it touches, at times our innermost existential paradoxes[125]. In one of her poems she says, When consciousness comes, body becomes unconscious/ Mind becomes leaves and leaves as I become conscious./'Sekh' says, those lovely songs of winter rendezvous/Suffering sings and sings as flute becomes conscious.[126]

What is also noteworthy in their poetry is the use of Hindu mythology—even lesser known episodes from the vast repertoire of Hindu tradition has been dealt with remarkable authenticity. Poems dedicated to Lord Shiva, Goddess Durga, Lord Krishna and Radha, Ram and Sita are replete with mythological references—some well known but some not so well known like Krishna going to Kundanpur to help Bhishm[127] or Shiva's role in Ganga's descent[128], are described with impressive credibility. It seems more striking and significant if we consider the present day's cultural unfamiliarity between Hindu-Muslim communities in India.

If we try to do close reading of poems and legends of our poetess, it may appear that Bhakti was, to some extent, an alternative way for escaping common day to day drudgery of their life in an orthodox social system of patriarchy. Taj says in one of her poems: *some may trusts on reading all four Vedas/some may trust on taking dip*

---

124 पैडो सम सूधो बैडो कठिन किवार द्वार /द्वारपाल नहीं तहां सबल भागति है ।'सेख' भनि तहां मेरे त्रिभुवन राय हैं जू./ दीनबंधु स्वामी सुरपतिन को पति है ।।वैरी को न बैरु बरियाई को न परबस /हीने को हटक नाही छीने को सकति है ।हाथी की हंकार पल पाछे पहुँचन पावै/चीटी की चिघार पाहिले ही पहुंचति है।। Aalam Granthavali, ibid, p.90

125 it is not possible to be agreed with Savitri Sinha's view that Sekh was mainly a poet of Sringar, see, Madhyakalin Hindi Kaviyatriyan, ibid, p.272

126 जब सुधि आवै तब तन बिनु सुधि होत/बनि सुधि आए मन होत पात पात है। / 'सेख' कहै सरद सहेट के वे गीत गुनि / बांसुरी की धुनि नटसाल गात गात है ।। Hindi ke Musalmaan Kavi, ibid, p.119

127 कुन्दनपुर जाय के सहाय करी भीष्म की /रूक्मिणी को टेक रखी लगी नहीं खाप है। ताज, Ibid, p.163

128 देखें सेख रंगरेजन की कविता गंगा वर्णन, शिव के प्रति, ibid p.114

into thousand streams of Ganga/'Taj', some may trust in worshipping all the Gods /some may trust on the remedy of magnanimous Shiva/ some may trust in finding paras to get mani /some may trust on troops of warriors/When in the world I've heard about saviour Krishna/I trust one and only this son of Nanda.[129]This unconditional trust by someone who is born and brought up in a different (i.e. historically rival) religious tradition can well be defined as a stance of disobedience or defiance towards conformity. In another poem she declares: *O son of Nand, I am lost to you/shall be with you dear like a devout hinduwani for you forever.*If we are conscious about the context of general Hindu-Muslim animosity of medieval times, declaration of this kind may be termed as truly rebellious:. In this way, Muslim women voice of Bhakti in pre-modern India is not a voice that conforms *Narada Bhakti Sutra's* dictum that *bhakti essentially is an elevation of "personal love,"*[130] rather it becomes, in some sense, political.

---

129 काहू को भरोसो वेड चारो जो पढ़े होत/काहू को भरोसो गंगा न्हाये सहस्त्र धार को/काहू को भरोसो सब देवन के पूजे 'ताज'/काहू को भरोसो विधि शंकर उदार को ॥/काहू को भरोसो मणि पाए मिले पारस को/काहू को भरोसो सूर वीरन के लार को /तारन के तरन कृष्ण सुने जो जहान बीच /मोको तो भरोसो एक नन्द के कुमार को ॥ ibid, pp.164-165

130 R. Raj Singh, Bhakti and Philosophy, Lexington Books, Lanham, 2006, p.83

6

Pre Colonial India & Dakkani

The culture evolved in Deccan during fifteenth to seventeenth century is unique in some way in the history of pre-colonial India. This can be cited as an example of the famous 'melting pot' characteristics of Indian civilization where different and sometimes opposing elements melting together into a harmonious whole resulting into a composite culture or it also may be interpreted as an illustration of how a homogeneous society becomes more heterogeneous through the influx of foreign elements of a different cultural background. Starting from Alauddin Khilji in 1294 to Asafjah in 1724 whoever invaded Deccan from the north, barring few all invasions were accompanied by thousand north Indian families, mostly Hindi speaking of Delhi, Bihar, Awadh and Rajasthan and Punjabi who subsequently settled there. With the emergence of Bahmani kingdom and especially in the time of Feroz(1397-1422) a new state policy of amalgamation has been initiated that was later reinforced in Baridshahi(1487-1619), Nijamshahi (1490-1633), Aadilshahi (1490-1683), and Kutubshahi (1512-1687) prominently. Arabic and Persian[131] remained the cultural language of Islam but a language called Dakkani was evolved by Sufis and Bhakta, kings

131 "...the influence of Persian culture was weaker in the south than in northern India; in fact, Arabic was more en vogue in the Deccan than Persian."Annemarie Schimmel, *Classical Urdu Literature from the beginning to Iqbal,* Otto Hararassowitz.Wiesbaden, 1975, p.131

and their courts, and common folks alike for their emerging needs of composite life and culture.

Sufi saints and Bhakta poets were the first to realize the potentialities of this newly emerging language, and it reminds the fact that exactly in the same situation, Awadhi was chosen by their counterparts in the north. Their primary concern was how to communicate with larger audiences since Persian and Arabic knowing gentries were very small; it was but natural that Hindui or Dakkani became their natural choice[132]. Shah Meeranji (d.1496) emphasizes this point, when he says: Vay Arbi bol Na janen, Na färsi pichhane /Yeh unko bachan hit sunnat boojhe reet (They do not know Arabic, or Persian. This is for their religious guidance)[133] Hindui or Dakkani, over the years became main medium of Sufi saints and Bhakti poets for its ability to Communicate more widely than any other language available to them, at that point of time. This was of course, not this language's ability of literary expression that mattered most for them[134] as Sufi works of Khwaza Bandanewaj Gesudaraj (1322-1423) Shah Meeranji Shamsul Ushaque (1408-1496) Shah Burhanuddin Janam (1544-1583) Aminuddin Alla (d.1675) and the Bhakti poetry of Namdev (c.1270-1350), Gondabai, (c.1300-1351) Eknath (1548-99), Tukaram

132 As per 1891 census, Dr. G.A.Grierson has mentioned 3654172 speakers of Dakkani in his *Linguistic survey of India*

133 "हमीं बोल अरबी करे |और फारसी बहुतेरे/यो हिन्दुवी बोले तब |इसका अर्ध भावे सब।यह भाषा भले सो बोले |पन इसका भाव खोले/वो अरबी बोल न जाने |न फारसी पछाने। श्रीराम शर्मा, दक्खिनी का पद्य और गद्य, हिन्दी प्रचार सभा, हैदराबाद, प्रथमावृत्ति १९५४, पृ.५२

134 "The Dakhni writings of all these mystics are important for philological rather than artistic reasons. These Sufis were not litterateurs in the true sense of the word; but, since they tried to approach large groups of the population they had to conform to the taste and mental capacity of their little learned followers in both form and content." Annemarie Schimmel, ibid, p137

(1608-49) keshav Swami(—1651) testifies it. Bandanewaj says in his *Chakkinama*, "Dekho vaajid tan ki chakki, peed chatur hoke sakki/ saukan iblish khinch khinch thakki, ke ya bismilla alla ho."[135] And Shah Meeranji in his *Khushnama:* "Khus khus häl khus khushiyaan khushi rahe bharpoor/ Yeh khus khushiyaan Allah karo anvarul Ali noor/ Phir wahi Jo prem lagave noor nishani ain/ Manjil ki sud lagave jahan dees Na rain."[136] Namdev proclaims, "Jinne janma dara hai tuj koon, bisar gaya unka dhyan joon/fir pastawega daga payega, nikal jayega awasan joo."[137] The process of amalgamation is very much evident here —not only the content but forms too are aspiring to break new grounds for common pursuit. It seems, it was conscious effort of Sufis to use not only their tested Arabic-Persian forms, genre or meter like Ghazals, Rubaees, Qasidas, Masnavis and Mustazad etc but dohas, geets, kavitts, ragas, raginis and other forms of Indian meters and folk-forms too. No wonder, as Richard M. Eaton found out that, "...until the twentieth century, when radio and cinema took its place, folk poetry of Sufi origin had occupied a dominant position in the folk culture of Deccan villages. The bulk of the folk poetry written by Sufis was sung by village women while engaged in various household chores. The most common types included the chakki-nama, so called because it was sung while grinding food grains at the grindstone or chakki, and the charkha-nama, sung while spinning thread at the spinning wheel, or charkha. Other types of such folk poetry included the luri-nama

---

135 "देखो वाजिद तन की चक्की |पीड चातुर होक सक्की || सौकन इब्लिस खिंच खिंच थक्की | के या बिस्मिल्ला अल्ला हो ||राहुल सांकृत्यायन, दक्षिणी काव्य-धारा, बिहार राष्ट्र भाषा परिषद्, पटना, 1959, p.3

136 Cited in Parmanand Panchal, Traditional Indian Forms of Deccani Poetry, Indian Literature, Vol. 53, No. 5 (253) (September/October 2009), pp. 211-219

137 जिन्नै जन्म डारा है तुज कूँ |बिसर गया उनका ध्यान जू ||फिर पस्तावेगा दगा पायेगा |निकल जायगा अवसान जू || श्रीराम शर्मा, वही, पृ.14

or lullaby, the shadi-nama or wedding song, the suhagan-nama or married woman's song, and the suhaila or eulogistic song."[138] This observation is quite in contrast to those views that proclaim that Dakkani Sufi narratives are more stylized and persianised, so less folk oriented or Indian than their counterparts in Awadhi premakhyans of the north.[139]Anyway folk literature of Dakkani reveals the same process and nature of amalgamation, what was at work in other areas of culture at that time. Let us discuss one folksong, that is popular mostly for singing in rainy season—it starts exclaiming that rainy season has arrived since flying clouds like black kites and water streams like silver thread are visible all over.[140]This beautiful imagery uses the word *abraan* for clouds that is Persian in origin but the feel of whole song is such that it hardly attracts your attention separately and this point is noteworthy.

It is said that, "the twin figures of the saint and the king occupied a central place in the cultural imagination of Muslims in premodern South Asia, just as parallel figures played key roles in Hindu as well as European written and oral literature."[141] Dakkani works produced side by side by the Sufi saints, Kings and their courts alike, especially in two newly independent principalities namely, Bijapur and Golconda, which later became main centre of Dakkani. The rulers of both the states were generous in patronizing

---

138 Richard M. Eaton, Sufi Folk Literature and the Expansion of Indian Islam, History of Religions, Vol. 14, No. 2 (Nov., 1974), p.119

139 देखे, परशुराम चतुर्वेदी, हिन्दी के सूफी प्रेमाख्यान, हिन्दी ग्रन्थ रत्नाकर, बंबई, प्रथम संस्करण, १९६२

140 "न्ह्योकाला आया न्ह्योकाला आया/उड़ते सो अबरा काले पतंगाँ/चांदी के डोरे पानी के धारां / न्ह्योकाला आया न्ह्योकाला आया/पानी की झाड़ियाँ मोती की लड़ियाँ /बादल के घोड़े सोने की छड़ियाँ/ न्ह्योकाला आया न्ह्योकाला आया" श्रीराम शर्मा, वही, पृ.३८८

141 Nile Green, Stories of Saints and Sultans: Remembering History at the Sufi Shrines of Aurangabad, Modern Asian Studies, Vol. 38, No. 2 (May, 2004), p.420

indigenous art and culture and Dakkani flourished here like nowhere else. It is also a fact that some rulers were themselves accomplice Dakkani poets and connoisseurs. Ibrahim Aadil Shah II (1556-1627) was one such ruler who not only himself a Dakkani poet of renown but musician, calligrapher and painter too. We know from Historian Farishta that he always used to speak in Dakkani and rarely in Persian[142], the court language of his time. This is the reason why Dakkani was 'recognized and cultivated as a national language in Golconda and Bijapur'.[143] Ibrahim Aadil Shah II was the first in Deccan to commission ragmala series of painting that developed in a distinct style of its own later[144]. He was also a master composer, guitar player and singer of dhrupad and his talent was remembered even by the Mughal emperor Jahangir (1569-27) in his autobiography.[145] His work *Kitab-e-Nauras* is very important since it is a book of dhrupad compositions with distinct literary acumen that also throws ample light on the general (including culture and language) policy of his reign. Book starts with a prayer to Saraswati, "Navras swar jag joti aani sarvaguni/yo sat Saraswati mata Ibrahim prasad bhayee duni."[146](O *Mother Goddess Saraswati, it is through your blessings on Ibrahim that the melodies and songs contained in Nauras will ever be cherished and will ever go on enlightening the wise musician.*) And then the first song of Bhupali raga describes Hazrat

---

142 http://www.thelibrarypk.com/tareekh-e-farishta/(accessed on 14.2. 2017)

143 Mohammad Sadiq, A History of Urdu Literature, Oxford University Press, Madras Calcutta Bombay, 1964, p.44

144 http://www.nybooks.com/articles/2015/06/25/renaissance-sultans/ (accessed on 20.2.2017

145 Henry Beveridge(ed.), Tuzuk-i-Jahangiri or Memoirs of Jahangir, Translated by Alexander Rogers, Royal Asiatic Society, London, 1909-1914, vol.i, p.134

146 "नवरस स्वर जगजोती आनी सर्व गुनी /यो सत सरस्वती माता इबराहीम प्रसाद भई दुनी"cited in Kitab-i-Nauras,(ed.) Nazir Ahmad, Sangeet Natak Akadami, 1956, p.95

Muhammad in these words, "Hazrat Muhammad Jagattar guru gosain/Tu dargah chumak meru man saar."*(Hazrat Mohammad is the preceptor of the world, His dargah is magnet and my heart is iron).*Out of fifty nine songs, nineteen are kannada ragas and only two foreign compositions,(Nauroz of khwarazmite tune and other Persian Hajiz)[147]and most of the songs describe Saraswati, Ganesh, Shiva and other Hindu deities. This catholic outlook of the rulers of Aadilshahi kingdom in Bijapur was also prevailed simultaneously in the Kutubshahi kingdom of Golconda, especially in the time and work of Muhammad Kuli kutub shah (r.1580-1611). Kuli kutub shah is considered to be the first poet of repute who has written in Dakkani, not for giving any instruction but out of pure creative compulsions. Literary Historian T. Grahame Bailey writes, "This royal poet ... deals with a great variety of subjects ... His love poems are truly Indian in style, not Persian. In addition to the usual subjects, beloved of Persian poets and their Urdu followers, he entered into matters of everyday life, describing Hindu and Muhamaddan feasts and festivals, celebrations of birth days and marriages, the customs prevailing in the country, life in his own royal palace, even fruits and vegetables, birds and flowers...It is astonishing that the first poet should have been so well equipped.[148]The power of poet's imagination can be gauged by the simple fact that some of his poems still move us. This song is still very popular for its simplicity and depth: "Piya baj pyala piya jaye na/piya baj ek til jiya jaye na/kahi the piya bin saburi karoon/ kahya jaye amma kiya jaye na/nahi ishq jis wah bada koodh hai/ kandhi usase mil besiya jaye na/kutubshah na de mujhe deevane

147 Ibid, p.68

148 T.Grahame Bailey History of Urdu Literature, Oxford University Press, London, 1932, p.20

koon pand/deewane koon kuch pand diya jaye na."[149]("without the loved one, wine cannot be drunk/Nor without her, one moment life be lived/They said: 'show patience absent from your love'/this can be said, but surely not be done/The man who knows not love is merciless/Never with such a one hold speech or sit/I am distracted, give me no advice/Never to such as I in counsel given."[150]).

Under the patronage and leadership of these two Deccan rulers, Aadilshahi and Kutubshahi court had attracted luminaries of various literary merits that consequently shaped the course of cultural dynamics. *Sabras* and *Qutb-Mustari* of Wajahi (1550-1609), *Chanda va Lorak* and *Tutinama* of Gauwasi (1620-?)'*Chand badan v mahiyar* of Muqimi, *Gulshane ishq* of Nusrati (d.1684) *Phulbadan* of Ibne Nishati these are, in some way, courtly works that were primarily the literary productions, meant to be stylized for the appreciations of connoisseurs but under the non-dogmatic environment their character became more fluid. One critic remarked, "The language is in a fluid state, drawing quite as freely on the indigenous element as on Persian and Arabic. Not only are Hindi phrases and expressions retained, there are Hindi and Persian and Persian and Hindi and Arabic compounds also. In the transcript of Persian and Arabic words the original spelling is often discarded in favour of a more phonetic spelling."[151]

Discarding original spelling in favour of a more phonetic spelling may be perceived as a metaphor for a process of amalgamation, a description for an evolutionary process of becoming a culture, composite; what we notice in the emergence of Dakkani —not only in an apparent form or style of a language, literature, architecture, painting, music but in a distinct way of living itself.

149 श्रीराम शर्मा, वही, पृ.७६

150 Tr.by T.Grahame Bailey, Ibid, p.21

151 Mohammad Sadiq, ibid, p.46

7

Colonialism and the Rise of Hindi Prose

It is said that when we engage with ourselves, poetry appears; but when we interact with others prose is born. The nature of colonialism in India is a highly contested issue but it can be safely argued that it has provided a kind of engagement where significant dialogue took place. And this very dialogue, it is true in some way that the evolution of prose in our country is somehow linked with. Sisir Kumar Das pointed out that: *Indian writers in the nineteenth century discovered, as it were, the potentiality and the possibilities of prose as an effective instrument of communication, both literary and non-literary. And in this discovery the initial impulses came from foreigners, Christian missionaries and the officials of the East India Company. The motivations of these foreign agencies were totally utilitarian: the interest of Christian missionary was to spread the word and the doctrines of Christianity; whereas the interest of the East Indian Company was to assure administrative efficiency. The college of fort William was established by Lord Wellesley to impart general education to the young British Civil servants...This was the first academic institution in India where both British and Indian scholars worked together. It gave a new direction to the civil service, initiated philological researches in various Indian languages, and started experiment with prose writing in Bengali, Urdu, Hindi and Marathi.*[152]

---

152 Sisir Kumar Das, A History of Indian Literature, vol.viii, Sāhitya Akademi, New Delhi, Reprint 1991, p.70

It is generally accepted that Indian prose during the course of evolution, had passed through three stages, namely, production of pedagogical materials, socio-religious debates and journalism[153] and in this regard Hindi prose is no exception. Initially the pedagogical materials were produced mainly by the institutions like Fort William College, School Book Societies of Punjab and Agra, Christian missionaries and by some distinct individuals like Raja Shiv Prasad *Sitarehind* (1824-1895), Raja Luxman Singh (1826 -1896), Navin Chandra Rai (1837-1890), etc.

The mandate given to Fort William College was unambiguous in its aim as its statutes, Framed by Wellesley clearly mentions that : *In as much as the college of fort William is founded on the principles of the Christian religion, and is intended not only to promote the knowledge of oriental literature, to instruct the students in the duties of the several stations to which they may be destined in the government of the British empire in India...but also to maintain and uphold the Christian religion in this quarter of the globe...*[154]Apart from the religious overtones, it differed completely from what the earlier education policy of East India Company had advocated through the activities of Asiatic society. Whereas a revival of ancient Indian learning was the outcome of earlier policy, Wellesley's policies were primarily for the living languages of India as he thought essential for public administration to know the language of the colonial subject. That's why the most important activity of the Fort William College was language teaching and related pedagogical publications were its corollary. As far as college's publications are concerned, 132 books in Arabic, Persian, Sanskrit, Punjabi, Hindi, Urdu, Bangla, Marathi, Telugu, and Kannada were prepared in which from the point of

---

153 Ibid, p.75

154 Quoted in Sisir Kumar Das, Sahibs and Munshis, Papyrus, Calcutta, Reprint 2001, p.23

evolution of Hindi -prose, *Premsagar* (1803) of Lallu Lal(1763-1824) and *Nasiketopakhyan*(1803) of Sadal Mishra are considered very significant. Although Hindi literary tradition was familiar with some prose works like Ram Prasad Niranjani's *Yogvashistha*(1741), Daulat Ram's *Jain Padmapuran*(1761), Sadasukh Lal (Niyaj)'s *Surasur nirnay(1783)* and Insha Alla Khan's *Rani Ketaki ki Kahani,* but Fort William College and Christian missionaries certainly gave a boost to it. *The Catalogue of Christian Vernacular Literature of India* intimates that there were thirteen major missions and societies which were actively engaged in producing Hindi tracts (exactly 255 in number), Books (59 in number) and periodicals (1) during 1846 to 1868.The total number of Hindi publications according to this catalogue is 315 excluding Roman catholic Publications as the compiler reported that *list of them could not be obtained without very great labour.*[155] Though predominantly these missions and societies were interested in spreading Christianity, they were also involved in preparing text-books for schools. It is true that their relations among various groups of protestants and roman Catholics were far from cordial and their relation with colonial power were also not always smooth, but mostly they worked in unison and with great missionary zeal. The pedagogical work they produced really helped the emerging vernacular prose to evolve and grow.

Pedagogical writings in Hindi were also done with equal enthusiasm and zeal by persons like Raja Shiv Prasad Sitarehind, Raja Luxman Singh and Navin Chandra Rai. The title of Raja to Shiv Prasad and Luxman Singh bestowed by the colonial power is also a significant point. It is a fact that both rajas got benefited from their colonial masters and if they collaborated with their

155 John Murdoch (compiled), Catalogue of the Christian vernacular literature of India, Caleb Foster Ptress, Madras, 1870, p.VI

language and other policies to some extent, it was but natural. No wonder Raja Shiv Prasad's *Itihas Timirnashak* (1864) follows closely the historiography of James Mill, especially in portraying medieval India as Dark Age.[156] But it is also true that Raja Shiv Prasad can truly be called the first major prose writer of Hindi as he not only published and edited the first Hindi newspaper in Hindi heartland (Banaras Akhbar, 1845) but strengthened the case of Hindi prose by writing and editing on almost all probable topics of his time—be it History (*Itihas Timirnashak: 1864, Shikhon ka Uday aur Ast: 1852*), geography (*Bhugol Hastamalak: 1855*), literature *(Gutka: 1870)* or natural sciences and so on. His prose was expressive enough to communicate with early aspirants of formal education and that was the reason his works became very popular, especially *Itihas Timirnashak*, along with Devkinandan Khatri (1861-1913)'s *Chandrakanta* (1891) was considered to be the most popular Hindi book of his times.F.E Keay pointed out that : *Raja Shiv Prasad (1823-1895) is especially remembered as one who tried to popularize a literary speech midway between the Persian ridden Urdu and the Sanskrit ridden High Hindi, which he believed to be nearer the colloquial speech of the people.*[157] Which language is *nearer the colloquial speech of the people* was the issue that was hotly debated in Hindi-Urdu controversy of 19th century. Comparing with the prose of Raja Luxman Singh, Literary Historian Ramchandra Shukla condemned *Sitarehind's* Persian ridden prose as *anti-natural and in passing he also hinted that it was done only to appease British officials.*[158]

---

156 See, James Mill, The History of British India, Pasternoster Row, Baldwin, London 1817

157 F.E Keay, A History of Hindi Literature, Asian Educational Services, New Delhi, Madras, Reprint 1989, p90

158 Ramchandra Shukla, Hindi Sahity ka Itihas, Nagri Pracharini Sabha, Varansi, 20th Reprint, 1983, p.299-300

What Raja Shiv Prasad *Sitarehind* had done in the eastern province of Banaras, in some respect, Navin Chandra Rai duplicated it in the western province of Lahore. Ramchandra Shukla observed: *What Raja Shiv Prasad, serving in education department had done to defend Hindi in United province, Babu Navinchandra Rai had been doing the same in Punjab. Not only had he written so many course-books in Hindi in between 1863 to 1880 but also made others to do the same. These books were prescribed there for so many years. He was among the first in Punjab to propagate women education. Apart from propagating education he was always involved in the activities of social reforms. It was already mentioned how Brahmo Samaj was established in Bengal to counter the Christian influence and Raja Rammohan Roy took Hindi too to propagate it. Navinchandra had started so many journals to propagate the ideas of Brahmo Samaj intermittently. In March 1867 he started one journal, called Jnandayani Patrika in which essays on education, general knowledge and science were also used to publish. Here it is important to mention that the Hindi with which he was involved in education department to propagate was pure Hindi prose*[159]. In *pure Hindi Prose,* purity refers to Sanskrit ridden High Hindi that was different from the so called Persian ridden *impure* prose! And this was the prose Shardha Ram Phillauri (1837-1881) was also using not only in his polemical discourses against Christianity throughout Punjab but in his novel (*Bhagyavati* and collections of essay (*Satyamrit-Pravah, Aatma-Chikitsa, Tattva Deepak, Upadesh – Sangrah)* too.

The growth of Hindi prose, in its initial phase was the product of 19th century colonial India where socio-religious, pedagogical, polemical writings and translations were need of the hour and apart from the name of Raja Shiv Prasad, Raja Luxman Singh,

159 Ibid, p.302

Navinchandra Rai, Shardha Ram Phillauri, the names of Ram Prasad Tripathi, Mathura Prasad Mishra, Brajvasi Das, Bihari Lal Choubey, Shivshankar, Kashi Nath Khatri and Ram Prasad Dubey are also worth mentioning in this regard.[160]The initial phase of this period was full of the vibrant activities pertaining to the emergence of powerful prose and modernity in India. Sisir Kumar Das notes: *The emergence of prose as a powerful medium brought a kind of change that coincided with the process of modernization. The modernization in Indian literature entails Indian endeavours towards adjusting itself with a foreign civilization. It is not westernization, as is commonly believed, but a response to the west.*[161] Here it may be added that the response was manifold as west meant so many things to so many people, but chiefly it was colonialism and Christianity that was picked vehemently to respond with. Brahmo Samaj and Arya Samaj were not only the pioneer voices of this response but pioneer medium of expression too. Raja Rammohan Roy (1774-1833) had chosen to express himself in English, Bangla, Hindi, Persian and swami Dayanand (1824-1883) Hindi and Sanskrit. It is not surprising that socio-religious debates that took place in 19th century journals were also the foundational texts of the emerging prose. Journals became the armory of the time and prose its main weapon. Hindi's first newspaper *Udant martand* by Pandit Jugal Kishore appeared in 1826 and Bangdoot in 1829 at Calcutta—both were weekly but Bangdoot was published in four languages—Hindi, Bangla, Persian and English and Ram Mohan Roy, Prince Dwarkanath Thakur and Prasanna Kumar Thakur were associated with it. In Hindi speaking area Shiv Prasad *Sitarehind's* Banaras Akhbar(1845,

---

160 Hazariprasad Dwivedi, Hindi Sahitya:Udbhaw aur vikas, Rajkamal Prakashan, Delhi. Reprint 1995, p.206

161 Sisir Kumar Das, A History of Indian Literature, vol.viii, ibid, p 78

Banaras), Taramohan Mitra's Sudhakar (1850, Banaras), Sadasukh lal's Buddhiprakash (1852, agra), Raja Luxman Singh's Praja-hitaishi(1861, Agra) Navinchandra Rai's Jnandayani Patrika(1867, Lahore) and Bhartendu's Kavivachan sudha(1867, Banaras) had played a major role in the evolution of Hindi Prose. The vigour with which sentiments and emotions were expressed in these papers and journals not only smoothened the initial shortcomings of the prose but made ways for further development.

8

Hardevi: The Forgotten Heroine of the 19th Century

Forgetting someone is like forgetting to turn off the light
In the backyard so it stays lit all the next day
But then it is the light that makes you remember.

(Yehuda Amichai)

When the Indian National Congress was formed in 1885, founding members like Mahadev Govind Ranade (1842-1901) and Raghunath Rao (1831-1912) expected that it would raise all social, economic and political issues, but soon they realized that some of the Congressman perceive social issues as a hindrance to political unity; Therefore, they laid the foundation of the National Social Conference, whose first session was held in Madras in 1887. Its purpose was to create a platform for mutual discussion regarding social issues. In the sixth National Social Conference of 1892, editor of *Bharat Bhagini* Smt. Hardevi (1859-1926), emphasized that the National Social Conference is more important than the Indian National Congress as "by the Indian National Congress the people hoped to get justice from the government. By the National Social Conference, they battered their social conditions. The justice which people expected at the hands of British government, ought to dispose them to do justice to those whose happiness and misery, joy and sorrow were intermixed with those of theirs. It is well said:

"The Women's cause is man's / They rise or sink together, /Dwarfed, or god-like, bond or free."[162] By quoting this poem of Tennyson, Hardevi was making her point quite clear as she was one of the few women intellectuals in the male-dominated society of North India who tried to improve the condition of widows and women's education in the late nineteenth and early decades of the twentieth century but the details of which are not recorded anywhere in the historiography of modern India, Hindi literary history also did not consider it appropriate to take cognizance of it, whereas her works like 'Stree Vilap' (1881), Seemantani Upadesh (1882), travel memoirs like 'London Yatra (1888) and 'London Jubilee (1889), novels like Hukmadevi (1892), treatise like Social Injustice on Women (1892)' are of great importance not only historically but from feminist point of view these are the early texts in hindi. For women education She started a magazines called 'Bharat Bhagini' (1889-1906), in Hindi and Urdu and established institution like *Nari Shilpalaya* (women Polytechnic:1902) for making women economically independent by imparting technical skills and laid the foundation of *Sundari Ashram* to provide shelters for helpless old people in Lahore. In nineteenth-century India when there were few examples of women-led societies, such as Pandita Ramabai (1958–1922)'s Arya Mahila Samaj (1882) in Pune or Swarna Kumari Devi (1855–1932)'s Sakhi Samiti (1886) in Calcutta, In 1885, Hardevi, along with Hemant Kumari Devi (1868-1953), formed the Vanita Buddhi-Vikasini Sabha in Lahore. She was one of the early advocates in introducing the Kindergarten system for child education in Punjab. She was also a pioneer in public oratory The *Bombay Guardian* records her public meeting in following

162 See, Vidya Dhar Mahajan, Modern Indian Political Thought, S.Chand & Company, New Delhi, First Edition 1987, p.176

words, "For an Indian lady who is an editor to stand up in a public meeting and delivered a lecture on the condition of Hindu Widows, and the practical means of its amelioration, would have been a an absolute impossibility a few years ago. But this is what happened in Bombay on Friday of last week, in the hall of the Prarthana Samaj, Girgaum. Mrs. Hardevi Roshan Lal, editor of the Bharat Bhagini of Lahore, delivered an interesting lecture in Hindi on 'the condition of Hindu widows and practical means of improving it.' She was listened to by an appreciative audience in which there were many Hindu ladies. Mrs. Madhavdas Raghunathdas, whose husband was so prominently identified with the movement for the amelioration of the condition of Hindu Widows, presided."[163] Similarly, when she was addressing a huge gathering in the Social Conference of 1893, the great reformer Gopal Ganesh Agarkar (1856-1895) declared it an elevating site.[164] At a time when women were hesitating even to step out of their houses, Hardevi not only raised the women issues from public forums with impunity, but throughout her life she was striving for its practical solutions—whether it was women's education, or the question of widow marriage or the issue of age of consent or the issue of women's hospital — she was very vocal, pro-active and determined in every matter.

We know very little about Hardevi's life, she has not revealed much about herself even in his travel memoirs —*London-Yatra* and

163 "Hindu Ladies Taking Part in a Public Meeting" in Blackburn, H.B. and Mackenzie, A.M. The Englishwoman's Review of Social and Industrial Questions, : Rutledge, London, 1902, p.27

164 Parimala V.Rao, Women's Education and the Nationalist Response in Western India, Indian Journal of Gender Studies, 15:1, 2008, p.142

London Jubilee. In a document of 1901, she was mentioned as 42 years old, so it seems, she born in 1859 AD. Her father's name was Rai Bahadur Kanhaiyalal (1820 -1888), who was quite renowned as a prominent engineer, historian and poet of Persian and Urdu. Rai Bahadur Kanhaiyalal was a resident of Jalesar in Agra district and completed his engineering from Rookie in 1851 and held the post of Executive Engineer in the Public Works Department of Lahore for thirty years, he was the first Indian to achieve that position. He was associated with the major renovation work of Mayo College of Art, Quaid-e-Azam Library, Dai Anga's Tomb, Sarfunisha Begum's Tomb, Jahangir's son Shahzada Parvez's Sangmarmari Tomb, Shahdara's Tomb of Jahangir and Asif Jaha etc. He also used to write professional articles on Indian engineering and some books he wrote in Hindustani for teaching rural students in engineering colleges. His Tarikh-e-Punjab and Tarikh-e-Lahore are his most important history books, in which he depicts facts imaginatively like a novelist. In 1868, Sir John Lawrence bestowed him the title of 'Rai' and in 1876, Viceroy Lord Northbrook (tenure 1872-1876) conferred him the title of 'Bahadur'. After retirement, the government also made him the president of the Lahore Municipal Corporation. He was also life member of the Senate of Lahore and Punjab University. He was also a good poet of Persian and his Masnavi *Nigrin Nama* on Heer Ranjha, Gulzare-Hindi and a work on the life of Maharaja Ranjit Singh are considered to be remarkable works. He was also interested in social reform and was one of the founding members of the Kayastha Dharma Sabha in Lahore. He had earned immense wealth from his talent and was soon considered among the wealthy peoples of Lahore. He had only two children—son Sewa Ram and daughter Hardevi. It is obvious that Hardevi must have brought up and educated in comfort but most of the accounts of that period mention only about her child-widowhood. However she herself tells the reader that she got married at the age of fourteen in her first work 'Stree Vilap'. She says: "Readers! Here I write about my marriage —

Prohit (priest) barber got me engaged in the greed of money in a house where neither the groom was good nor there was anything worthful in the house. At that time I was fourteen years old, I was aware of the meaning of groom and marriage. When someone said that there is a good groom, then I used to be happy, when someone described that the groom is not good, then I felt frustrated but would keep mum in my heart. When the time of marriage came and the wedding procession reached near my home, then I overheard onlookers saying that the bridegroom is absolutely unworthy of the girl.so at that time my heart was filled with a longing to see the bridegroom so much that only I know, but I did not see any option but to weep for the lives of the brothers of Kali Yuga, there is a custom in our community that when the marriage procession comes to the door, then a female barber takes the girl in her lap and throws rice in her mouth on the groom seven times, as soon as the female barber opened my mouth to spit the rice, considering the time as an opportunity, I observed the groom well.

"But at that time I did not have the intelligence to evaluate but were able to recognize beauty and ugliness quite well, as soon as I saw it, I drowned in the river of sorrow, but I could not find any shore except patience. People were celebrating, no one knew the condition of my heart. I was not liking food, clothes, jewelry but my parents and relatives thought that my condition was due to impending separation.

"Then when my father held my hand and gave it to the bridegroom at the time of bride- donation, I wanted very much not to let hold my hand, but I started crying helplessly and could not say anything, as if an innocent is being taken to be hanged.

"So only God knew my condition, neither could I tell anyone, nor was anyone able to understand at that time, then on the day of farewell, I started looking at the bridegroom from a window in a faraway corner and used to say in my heart that Alas! My father's intelligence is completely destroyed, alas! At this time no one explains to my father, hi! God, how will I spend my whole life with this man, which my eyes now do not accept, if you had created such a groom for me in the world, then do not make my life too long so that I can get rid of sorrows soon, ha! Barber priests, May God take revenge on you! My father gave a lot of dowry, very beautiful ornaments of precious gems, very nice clothes, money, Ashrafi, ferry, house, garden, land etc. Made Swami very rich, but all these things did not make me happy at all, but on the contrary, all these things became the reason for my sorrow. If my father had married me with my consent, I would have been more happy than not giving these valuables to me, because even if someone becomes the king of the whole world but has pain in his heart, he remains unhappy like hell and If the heart is not worried about pain, then even hell speaks as soothing as heaven."[165]

This autobiographical piece is the voice of a personality who values woman's freedom in a patriarchal society and who does not consider the mere comforts and conveniences as happiness and is also aware of her rights, but unfortunately could not be able to challenge her own marriage that was arranged without her consent

165 Hardevi, *Stree Vilap*.Shahjahanpur: Arya Darpan Press, 1881, p.13-15

and possibly this may be the reason that the writer has not revealed her name in the book, rather it was mentioned on the cover as a work by a 'Tormented Grieving Widow.'

In the same year in 1881, 'On the condition of Hindu widows', she delivered a poignant lecture in Prarthana Samaj, Bombay, whose echoes were reverberated far and wide. Addressing to the women in audience, she strongly advocated the widow-remarriage in a tone which had passion of her own sufferings and rationality of a social reformer. This speech became so famous instantly that not only it was translated into Marathi and published in the Prarthana Samaj's mouthpiece Subodh Patrika (7 August 1881) but When the second edition of Baba Padmanji (1831-1906)'s Yamuna Paryatan, arguably the India's first novel, was published in 1882, this lecture was included in its appendix, for the novelist argued that Yamuna, the heroine of the novel, has been authenticated by this lecture. In its next edition (the third edition of Yamuna Paryatan, 1889), another article by Hardevi was included in the appendix, saying that it proves that how untrue the novel was accused of exaggerated depiction of widow life![166] According to the novelist Baba Padmanji, this article was translated from the April 1889 issue of the English magazine, *'The Gospel in All Lands'*. This was the same article that was published in the November 1881 issue of the Journal of the National Indian Association under the title 'Hindu Widows by One of Them', Written by 'a Young Widow, and Translated by an English Lady'[167]. Both these articles from Marathi have been translated into English by Maya Pandit and compiled in 'Women Writing in India'

---

166 Padmanji B. *Yamunaparyatan.Pune: Snehvardhan* Prakashan, 2005, 10-12 &111-112

167 Hardevi, 'Hindu Widows by one of them' in *Journal of the National Indian Association,* 121, 1881, pp.624-630

edited by Susie Tharu and K.Lalitha.[168] The fame of this article was such that when Devendra N. Das wrote an article titled 'The Hindu Widow' in the Nineteenth Century magazine, he not only quoted a part of it but the whole argument was also based on it. He concluded the article by saying, "I cannot conclude this description of the treatment of Hindu widows in the North - West Provinces of India without quoting some of the burning words of one of them, which were translated by an English lady and published in the Journal of the National Indian Association for November 1981: Why do the widows of India suffer so? Not for religion or piety. It is not written in our ancient books, in any of the Shástras or Mahabharata. None of them has a sign of this suffering. What Pandit has brought it upon us? Alas! That all hope is taken from us! We have not sinned, then why are thorns instead of flowers given us? Thousands of us die, but more live. I saw a woman die, one of my own cousins. She had been ill before her husband's death; when he died she was too weak and ill to be dragged to the river. She was in a burning fever; her mother in-law called a water -carrier and had four large skins of water poured over her as she lay on the ground where she had been thrown from her bed when her husband died. The chill of death came upon her, and in eight hours she breathed her last. Every one praised her and said she died for love of her husband. I knew another woman who did not love her husband, for all their friends knew they quarreled so much that they could not live together. The husband died, and when the news was brought the widow threw herself from the roof and died. She could not bear the thought of the degradation that must follow. She was praised by all. A book full of such instances might be written. The only difference for us

168 Tharu S. &Lalita K, *Women Writing in India* Delhi: Oxford University Press, 1991, pp. 356-358

since sati was abolished is, that we then died quickly if cruelly, but now we die all our lives in lingering pain. We are aghast at the great number of widows. How is it that there are so many? The answer is this, that if an article is constantly supplied and never used up it must accumulate. So it is with widows; nearly every man who dies leaves one, often more; though thousands die, more live on. The English have abolished sati; but, alas! Neither the English nor the angels know what goes on in our houses, and Hindus not only don't care but think it good![169] Similarly Pandita Ramabai in her fifth chapter of 'The High Caste Hindu Woman' (1887), also cites this article thoroughly to prove the veracity of her statement and she also used Hardevi's 'The Prayer of Aryan Women' (Arya Striyon Ki Prarthana), considering it in the present context more appropriate than her own words.[170] Both these works — 'The Prayer of Aryan women' and 'Torture To Destitute' (Rando Par Sitam) are included in Hardevi's 'Women's Sermon' (Seemantani Upadesh) which was published on February 1st, 1882 but again she did not mention author's name but simply writes 'A Hindu Woman'. What could be the reason for hiding her name? There is a long debate around this question in Hindi literary world.[171] The way Hardevi remembered her father and the radical manner in which she raised the issue of widows and their remarriage, the question arises whether the elite society of the nineteenth century was receptive enough for this, especially when the writer had an ambition to make her life a

---

169 D.N. Das, 'The Hindu Widow' in The Nineteenth Century, XX:364-372, 1886, pp. 364-372

170 Ramabai, *The High Caste Hindu Woman*, Fleming H. Revell Company, New York, Chicago Toronto: 1901, pp. 114 &111

171 See, Dharmaveer (ed.) Simantani Upadesh, Vani Prakashan, New Delhi; 1999, pp.38-40 and Charu Singh, 'Agyaat Hindu Stree Kaise Banti Hai' in Alochana, 58, 2016, pp.15-44

message? Could it be more than just a coincidence that no work was published by her name during her father's lifetime? Bipin Chandra Pal writes in his Memoirs (1932): "we came to know during our sojourn in Lahore the late Mr. Sevaram, son of the millionaire Rai Bahadur Kanhaiya Lal. Sevaram went to England with his wife and his widowed sister to finish his education. He helped the later to remarry Roshanlal, Bar-at-law. This was against the wishes of his father and it created a painful misunderstanding between father and son."[172]It is also a fact that Hardevi's remarriage was not made known to her mother.[173] The authorship of her two early works—-Widow's Laments' (Vidhwa Vilap) and 'Women's Sermon' (Seemantani Upadesh) was revealed and authenticated by a review of her book Tameel-e-Teeflan which appeared in the July 1889 issue of *The Indian Magazine* with following titles: "Talīm-e-Teeflan (Kindergarten): The Instruction of Children; or, The Treasure of Instruction By Smt. Hardevi, daughter of Rai Bahadur Kanhaiya Lal, Oriental Press, Lahore, 1889. The reviewer mentions clearly in following words: "The authoress of this book seems determined to make herself conspicuous by devotion to the cause of female education in India. Her former works, such as *Simantani Sangit, Vidhwa Ashru, Simantani Upadesh, London Jubilee, and London Yatra* were thoughtfully books, and all were intended to awaken reflection and enquiry among Indian women."[174] In the above list of books, Simantani Sangit (women's music) is still unknown and 'Vidhwa Ashru' (widow's tears) could be another title for 'Stree

---

172 Bipin Chandra Pal, *Memories of My Life and Times*, UBS Publishers. New Delhi, 2004, p.397

173 Sant Nihal Singh 'A Long Distance Intellectual Companion' in *Sachchidananda Sinha Commemoration Volume* Patna: The United Press LTD, 1947, p.4

174 The Indian Magazine, Kegan Paul, Trench & Co. London, 1889, p.316

Vilap' (Female lamentation) and rest of the later works— Striyon Pe Samajik Anyay (1892) and Hukum Devi (1893) are known and documented.

Hardevi was amongst the first woman from Hindi region to go to London. At that time many newspapers and journals in English and Hindi made it headlines. The news of her going to London along with Dadabhai Naoroji, Ratan Banerjee, Lakshmi Narayan and her brother Sevaram's family was reported in *The Indian Magazine,* Their reception on their arrival in London was also reported in The Indian Magazine titled 'A Welcome to the Newly Arrived Hindu Ladies in London'. Khushvakt Rai reports in these words: "I cannot help expressing the pleasure and rejoicing that we feel on the important occasion of the arrival, on the 5th of April, of two Hindu ladies in England.

"The arrivals are, Mr. and Mrs. Seva Ram and their daughter, a little child, and Srimati Hardevi, His sister, from the Punjab. We could not give a grand reception, as we proposed, on account of the uncertainty of our friend's arrival. By my using the expression "Welcome to the Hindu Ladies, "I hope the gentleman, Mr. Seva Ram and Mr. Lukshmee Narain, will not think that we do not welcome them. The reason why I have put the ladies in the first instance is, that they are the only and first Kayusth ladies from the N.W.P or the Punjab who crossed the sea."[175]

The stay in London brought a turning point in Hardevi's life—- not only did she document her journey from Lahore to London

175 Khushvakt Rai, A welcome to the newly arrived Hindu Ladies in London in *The Indian Magazine*, C.Kegan Paul, London, 1886, p.276.

here but also recorded the birth anniversary of Queen Victoria in London-Yatra and London Jubilee respectively, but soon after reaching London she began to study the England's teaching systems of the schools. She writes: "I have always taken very great interest in the education of the Indian people; but educational institutions in India are comparatively few, and as yet not properly and well organized. The "parda system" in our country is no small impediment to the growth and development of female education there. Girls' schools, therefore, in India are but exceptions to the general rule. When I arrived this country last year, my curiosity to see Ladies' schools here was very great; and I now possess the satisfaction of having seen at least something of many such private institution of England. "[176] She presents these experiences in her book *Talime-Tiflan* after returning to India.

Another incident of her stay in London which turned her life upside down was her love for Roshan Lal. Reminiscing those days, eminent journalist and family-friend Sant Nihal Singh writes that, "Love, however entered her young breast. Tradition sought to nip it in the bud it whispered into her ear.

"A widow has no concern with love. Pluck it out, root and branch"

"She had good cause to know that, in this matter, tradition was, for a high caste Hindu girl like herself, inflexible it was, indeed, no less inexorable than the laws of our Iranian neighbors and cousins, the Medes and Persians.

"Har Devi did not wince nor quail. She gathered all the resources within her to defy the tradition.

176 Hardevi, 'An Indian Lady upon the True Basis of Social reform' in *The Indian Magazine*, September, 1887, London, pp.482-487

"Defy it she did. Successfully."[177]

She got married and this news flashed prominently in various newspapers. Hindustani (Lucknow) dated 21st September 1890, titled 'Marriage of Lala Roshan Lal, Barrister-at-Law with Miss Hardevi, a widow,' "referring to the marriage of Lala Roshan Lal, B.A. Barrister–at-law, Allahabad with Miss Hardevi, the widowed daughter of late Rai Bahadur Kanhaiya Lal of Lahore, observes that it is an advocate for the marriage of Hindu widows; particularly of those among them who become widows in their childhood. But the times are not yet ripe for the introduction of such a new custom, and the mere mention of widow marriage is generally regarded with abhorrence and horror. Social reform should be introduced slowly, in as much as any sudden and radical changes are calculated to injure rather than promote it. Lala Roshan Lal was very fortunate that, on his return from England, he was received back into society by his caste fellows without being required to undergo any penance according to the Hindu religion. He should not have married a widow, particularly one belonging to a different community. He is a Saksaina Kayastha, while Miss.Hardevi is a Bhatnagar; and inter-marriages are not allowed between those classes of Kayasths. He is sure to be excommunicated on account of the marriage. Miss. Hardevi is a good Sanskrit and English scholar and publishes a Hindi monthly journal. Her marriage will give a rude shock to the cause of female education, as it will lead ignorant Hindus to imagine that education has a bad effect on women."[178] *The Hamdard*, Fyzabad of the 24th September, 1890 expresses nearly the same sentiments on the subject.

---

177 Sant Nihal Singh, ibid, p.3

178 Compiled as "Marriage of Lala Roshan Lal",) in *The Indian Magazine and Review*. 1892, pp. .264:660

The way this reporting is presented, shows the sentiments of the time and it is clear that the phenomenon of widow remarriage was uncommon at that point of time, the menace of which has not subsided even fifteen years later as in a column of the *Hindustan Review*—'A Widow Marriage in High Life'—-reveals: "It is now nearly Fifteen years since the announcement that Mr. Roshan Lal, Bar-at-Law, had married Srimati Hardevi— daughter of the distinguished Engineer, the late Rai Bahadur Kanhaiya Lal of Lahore —startled the Hindu community of Upper India in general and the Kayastha community in particular. The news, in fact, came like a bombshell and produced regular consternation in the community. Even those who in their hearts approved of the marriage felt themselves compelled by force of circumstances to denounce Mr. Roshan Lal and the defunct Kayastha Gazette of Bankipur—-the conductors of which were man of liberal views and progressive tendencies —entered into a vigorous polemical campaign against Mr. Roshan Lal."[179]

Bareilly resident Roshanlal (1858-1932) returned to India from London in 1887 after completing Bar-at-law and after a year in 1888, Hardevi also returned from London, when she got the news of father Kanhaiya Lal's sudden death. At that time except parents all the four members of the family —Hardevi, her elder brother Sewaram, sister-in-law and niece Radhika —were in London, all returned immediately to Lahore. Sewaram and his wife's bar-at-law courses in London were not yet completed, so after the funeral they went back again. Hardevi remained in Lahore with her mother. Brother Seva Ram returned after a year but suddenly he died in Calcutta. He was not only Hardevi's elder brother but also her true

179 "A Widow-marriage in High Life." in *The Hindustan Review*, Allahabad, The Indian Press, 1906,

well-wisher, guide and friend, he translated many of her articles into English and got them published in the Indian Magazine. Going against father's wish, he also supported her proposed marriage to Roshan Lal. After Seva Ram's death, his only daughter Radhika Devi (1880–1919) was married to Mr. Sachchidanand Sinha (1871–1950) in 1894, who later became one of the architects of modern Bihar. Sachchidanand Sinha used to come to Lahore to meet her every year during holidays and that was continued even after the death of Radhika Devi in 1919. He had great respect for Hardevi and was great admirer of her work. Roshanlal Saxena, However, after returning from London in 1887, started practicing in the Allahabad High Court. He was an Arya Samajist since his school days. He was also a social reformer, used to give lectures for abstinence and cow protection, He had many contacts outside his province as well, especially with the Hindu Sabha of Lahore. He was a bitter critic of the American Zenana Mission in Allahabad and probably that is the reason he took an active part in establishing the Girls High School there. After marriage, he remained in Lahore. According to *Arya Lekhak Sangh,* he was elected a member of the Philanthropist Sabha in 1896. He was also the head of the Arya Samaj Bachhowali Lahore and minister and deputy head of the *Arya Pratinidhi Sabha,* Punjab. He also wrote two books—*A Fingerpost to the Religion of the Vedas* and *Stray Thoughts on the Arya Samaj.* He was fully committed to the principles of Arya Samaj—even to the extent that he opposed the Age of Consent bill against the known opinion of his Brahmo wife Hardevi.[180] Durga Prasad, the English translator of Maharishi Dayanand Saraswati's famous work *Satyarth Prakash*, dedicating his work to Roshanlal in 1908, wrote: "The first and foremost in Kayesth Social Reform To Rai

180 Lucy Carol Stout, *The Hindustani Kayastha: The Kayastha Pathshala, and the Kayastha Conference, 1873-1914*, University of California, Berkeley, 1976, p.154

Roshan Lal Sahib, B. A.Barrister-at-Law, Lahore, Punjab, and a true friend of the Arya Samaj, whose charitableness of disposition and suavity of manners render him very amiable to all his friends and whose earnest zeal and sincere love of Indian Reformation is so well known to all, is this humble tribute to the sacred memory of Maharishi Swami Dayanand Saraswati in the shape of an English Translation of the Satyarth Prakash, the masterpiece of his works, dedicated as a token of gratitude For his lending a large sum of money to bring out this book without any security whatever on the recommendation of Babu Gopal Chander, B. A. Pleader, Lahore, by the Translator Durga Prasad, Lahore 1908."[181] However it is also known that he was excommunicated for marrying Hardevi, a Bhatnagar Kayastha widow, while a few days earlier, his sea voyage was overlooked.[182] Remembering those days of Lahore, Saint Nihal Singh has written that, "The Roshan Lal then lived in a house that the Rai Bahadur Kanhaiya Lal had expressly built for Har Devi near his own. It was a gathering point for young man mostly students from the colleges who considered themselves to be progressive Soon this place became a meeting place for the youth—especially for those college students who considered themselves progressives, I in my 'undergrad' days, so regarded myself.

"Hardevi was to us a heroine.

"This is not the place to ponder the mental struggles that must have been the high caste Hindu lady a prior to her consenting to bestow her hand upon that young man. Roshan Lal seemed never to have had any qualms about the union .For him the world held

181 Durga Prasad, *An English Translation of Satyarth Prakash*, Virjanand Press, Lahore, 1908

182 C.A. Bayly,) *The Local Roots of Indian Politics, 1880-1920*. Clarendon Press, Oxford, Great Britain, 1975, pp.116-117

only one women —Har Devi. He married her by Arya Samaj rites, in 1891 in Lucknow where after his return, he first set up practice. She remained his whole world till she died in 1926.He himself lived on disconsolate, till 1932."[183]

Hardevi's activism in the public sphere was lifelong. Since she was more inclined to social issues than political, it is difficult to find any direct anti-colonial stance in her life and letters — rather at some places there is admiration for British rule and Queen Victoria, but there is also evidence when "She arranged meetings and collected funds for the purpose of assisting anarchists under trial"[184]. and the Criminal Intelligence Department, reported in 1908 about women's 'increasing interests in politics' when "Sarla Devi and Hardevi were the most prominent women leaders of this time. They organized secret associations, collected funds for revolutionary under trial prisoners and arranged meetings to inculcate the national spirit amongst the women and youth of the region."[185]Besides, it is certain that she devoted most of her time to social issues concerning women and It is also true that whoever raised the women's question from whatever platform, irrespective of their ideology, Hardevi supported them and welcomed them whenever they came to Lahore—be it Lady Dufferin (1843 -1936) or Miss. Manning (1828-1905), or Shivnath Shastri (1847-1919) and his daughter Kamini Rai. Lady Harriet Dufferin, wife of Viceroy Lord Dufferin, had done incomparable work in the field of women's health in India, for which a women's delegation went to her official

---

183 Sant Nihal Singh, ibid, pp.4-6

184 M. Kaur, *Role of Women in the Freedom Movement, 1857-1947*. Sterling Publishers, New Delhi, 1968, P.98

185 M.Singh, History and Culture of Punjab, Atlantic Publishers and distributors. New Delhi, 1989, P.248

residence and gave her a citation; the secretary of the delegation Hardevi read the citation there (Lady Dufferin at Lahore 1989:89). Hardevi also held a meeting at her home in honor of Lady Dufferin in December 1888, which was attended by 150 veiled women and which was declared by the press as the first of its kind in Lahore. (Indian Intelligence1888:658) Similarly, when Elizabeth Adelaide Manning (1828–1905), who took the National Indian Association to a new height after the death of Marie Carpenter (1807–1877), visited India, Hardevi invited at her home to welcome in Lahore.[186] Perhaps Miss Manning was the one who translated her work as 'An English Lady'. Similarly, when Shivnath Shastri arrived in Lahore with his daughter Kamini Sen, Hardevi along with her brother Sewaram and sister-in-law were among those who welcomed them at the station. According to the Tribune, "The Pundit was received at the railway station by many Brahmins and other friends. Mr. Seva Ram, among others was there to receive him. The ladies were received by a number of Bengali and Punjabi ladies, among whom were Mrs. Seva Ram and Srimati Hardevi."[187]when Behramji Merwanji Malabari's (1853-1912)'s *Notes on Infant Marriage and Forced Widowhood*, was discussed widely in the country, she took active interest in it and subsequently thanked when the government raised the age of consent from ten to twelve years .It was reported in *Indian Magazine* as such:, "Srimati Hardevi, in an effective speech, said that she had long urged that government should help to prevent early marriages, and that she was rejoiced that the proposed measure had now become law. On several occasions she

186 "Miss Manning at Lahore" (1889) The Indian Magazine, Kegan Paul, Trench & Co. London, p. 167

187 "Indian Intelligence" The Indian Magazine, Kegan Paul, Trench & Co. London, 1889, p.656

had written on the subject in the Indian Magazine (then called the *Journal of the National Indian Association*). She referred to the earnest labours in this cause of Mr. B.M.Malabari, and expressed her confidence in the sympathy of the Indian Government with regard to social questions."[188] She was also very much active in the activities of National Social Conference from the very beginning and when the fourteenth conference was held in Lahore in 1900, she vigorously participated and raised the issue of women's education effectively. The report of the proceedings, quoting *Purity Servant* says that, "The speeches of Lalas Sunder Suri, Hansraj, Shiv Dayal, Ruchi Ram, Lajpat Rai, Bishan Narayan Razdan, Diwan Narinder Nath and Munshi Ram were excellent. But Shrimati, Hardevi the gifted wife of Mr. Roshan Lal excelled all. She was entrusted with the first resolution on Female Education and she put the men to shame for having neglected the education of women .We had never expected that she would be able to speak so admirably. Roshan Lal is a good speaker and as president of the reception committee he performed his part well but we must gloriously confess that he was overshadowed by his better half. Our congratulations are to the noble pair. The persecutions and troubles to which they have often been subjected for their noble and practical advocacy of social reform will be illustrations of encouragements to the younger generations. May they be long spared in our midst to carry on their work of usefulness is our prayer."[189] It is interesting to note that by the beginning of the twentieth century Hardevi became so well known for the cause of women's awakening that when Bandaru Acchamamba (1874-1904), the first feminist historian of India

188 "Indian Intelligence" The Indian Magazine, Kegan Paul, London, Trench & Co.1891, p.322

189 The Fourteenth Indian National Social Conference, 1900, p.5

from remote Andhra, edited *Abala Saccharitra Ratnamala* (A Garland of Great Women's Life Histories: 1901), she considered necessary to include her name.[190] In later years, she started participating in the Swadeshi movement along with Sarla Devi's Bharat Stree Mahamandal (1910). Mahatma Gandhi wrote in Young India, July-November 1920: "The joint secretaries of the Bharat Strī Maha Mandal, Punjab branch send a report of the Swadeshi activities of Shrimati Sarla Devi Chaudhrani ever since her return to Lahore from Bombay. Miss Roy and Mrs. Roshanlal the Secretaries, state that meetings of women were held respectively on 23rd, 24th and 25th June at three different places in Lahore."[191] Now Indian history was entering an another phase where social change was not perceived through bill and legislation with cooperation of the government rather the political strategy of non-cooperation and civil disobedience was going to be enforced. The earlier agenda of the social conference was all included in Gandhi's Congress; It is not surprising that now on, the voices of people like Hardevi are less prominent in the documents of this period, probably their role had been completed.

Hardevi has expressed gratitude to four great men as women-saviors in *Seemantani Upadesh*, they are: Munshi Kanhaiyalal Alakhdhari (1809–1882), Pandit Shiv Narayan Agnihotri (1850–1929), Naveen Chandra Rai (1837–1890) and Swami Dayanand Saraswati (1824–1883) (Hardevi 1882:44).The authoress says that all the women of India should pay their obeisance to them, rather

190 See, Tharu S. &Lalita K. *Women Writing in India* Delhi: Oxford University Press.1993, p.324

191 Swadeshi in the Punjab, young India, 1920, p.20

consider them as an incarnation of God. This choice, it seems a reflection of her personal preference but also could be an effective strategy for the cause of women's emancipation in her times.

Nineteenth century India was restless —- engulfed with churning of problems, solutions, searching, researching, debates, arguments, etc. Such moments are considered to be creative. Kenneth W. Jones has shown in his study that how the interaction of North-Western society with the British colonial culture created a third world of marginalized people, that began first in Delhi during the 1830s and 1840s, but was terminated abruptly by the mutiny. The process began anew in the Punjab proper during the 1860s and 1870s, not so much as a group phenomenon but as an individual one. Men such as Kanhaiya Lal Alakhdhari existed as loners, prophets of a future not yet arrived. Not until the 1880s did the Punjab produce its first generation of marginal men, youths educated in the English language who supplied sufficient manpower to sustain movements for change. They sought new ideas and found them in the Brahmo Samaj, Dev Dharma and Arya Samaj."[192] Hardevi has written in verse about Kanhaiya Lal Alakhdhari in her first work Stree Vilap: "When the Alakhdhari was absorbed in my mind,/ the phantom shadows vanished from my head./ The sun of knowledge when arose,/ the glory of phantom shadow melted"(Hardevi 1881:2). It was Alakhdhari who also got Hardevi's *Seemantani Upadesh* published. Hardevi also had a close relationship with Brahmo Samaj and Arya Samaj, Pandit Shivnarayan Agnihotri was also an outspoken member of Brahmo Samaj, later for some personal and ideological reasons established a separate Dev Dharma. Babu Navinchandra Rai who was among

---

192 K.W. Jones, *Arya Dharm Hindu Consciousness in 19*th *-Century Punjab,* Manohar Publishers and Distributors. *Delhi*, 2006, p.314

the founders of Brahmo Samaj in Lahore and his daughter Hemant Kumari Chaudhrani had personal family relations with Hardevi and it is also reported that when the elder brother Sevaram was excommunicated from the caste as a punishment for sea voyage, he also entered the Brahmo Samaj and Husband Roshan Lal was well known Arya Samajist. In this way Hardevi had a close relation with the radical reformist stream of the North-West Province and it is not accidental that Hardevi's entire life and letters happen to be in opposition to *Sanatani* world-view.

Shardha Ram Phillauri (1937-81) was the representative of the Sanatani way of life in the North-Western Provinces. Arguing with Kanhaiya Lal Alakhdhari, Shardha Ram says that hard work should be done to protect the Hindu religion, but only those men can protect it, who first become a staunch Hindu himself, although all of us are claimants of Hinduism, however A true Hindu is one who considers the commandments of *Shruti* and *Smriti* to be true and accurate. If by considering the order of Vedas and Dharma Shastra as mere construction of Brahmins and considering any other subtle matter as Hindu religion, then he cannot be a Hindu. if I am forgiven, I would like to say one thing that Alakhdhari Sahib neither do you wear braids on your heads nor the sacrificial thread around your neck, which Vaishyas definitely need as per the commandments of Shruti and Smriti and being disgusted by cow dung, you take your food on table by calling it *khana*, not *bhojan* and consider untouchability, caste, etc. as useless, then How it is possible from such a person to expect the growth of Hinduism? Then, in his writings, most of the pieces are filled with such ideas as it is foolish to worship the incarnations of Krishnachandra, Ramchandra etc. and the gods like Brahma, Vishnu etc., pilgrimage like Ganga, Yamuna etc. and idols and Charity, donations to various offerings for religious rituals are constructs of Brahmins for exploiting and robing the world. Then he wants to listen Vedas and Shastras in front of Muslims and Christians wearing shoes and cannot even support the tilak applied on someone's forehead, then how can he protect Hindu religion?"[193] Shardha Ram took on the reformists— Babu Navin Chandra Rai, the founder of Brahmo Samaj in Lahore and Swami Dayanand, the founder of Arya Samaj—-in Punjab with this kind of Sanatani logic and zeal. The struggle between the *Sanatanis* and the reformists was, in fact a conflict of faith versus conscience or tradition versus modernity. Kanhaiya Lal Alakhdhari, the centre of Shraddharam target is the one who publishes works like *Simantani Upadesh* for better understanding for women and for whom Hardevi says, Kanhaiya Lal Alakhdhari 'whose single word is not without value. Wrote many books and published various magazines. There is not a single book in which there is no plea for the release of these women prisoners.'[194] It is true that traditional (Sanatani) thinking, instead of breaking fetters, has been always exhorting to consider it as flowers, Hardevi argues, "In Mahabharata, Manusmriti etc. of Hindus, there is no other virtuous hymn for women other than that of husband is written. Ved Vyas, Parashar, Vashishtha, Markandeya, Yajnavalkya, Valmiki, all have prescribed husband-worship (Pativrat Dharma) as the main religion for women. Women get all the benefits of worshiping God by worshiping their husband. The siddhis that sages get by doing great penance, she gets it simply by serving her husband..."[195]It is interesting to know that Almost all the male writers of Bhartendu -era are convinced of this opinion. Pratap Narayan Mishra

193 Dev, ***Shraddhaprakash***, Punjab Economical Press, Lahore, 1896, p.30

194 Hardevi, Seemantani Upadesh, 1882, p.44

195 Ibid, p.105

(1856-1894) is so eager to teach the lesson of husband-worship to women that he says, "Women are now especially stupid. Therefore, it would be better to deal with them by applying Sam (cunningness), Dam (pricing), Dand (punishment) and Bhed (flattering). They will not return on track by mere law and nature. They should be treated in such a way that they remain happy and afraid simultaneously. Only then will they love. They can only be afraid of stalking as Kanaujis do, but they will not love. Even if they are given pure freedom as Agarwals and Khatris do, they will be arrogant. Therefore, it is advisable to make them realize both fear and love, independence and dependence simultaneously. Keep on giving permission and education, and sometimes keep taking their advice as well is the key. Only with these measures it is possible that the girls of India will start leaning towards husband worshiping again and due to this our fortune will shine once again."[196] Now it is useless to comment upon this, but see what Hardevi has to say about *Pativrat-dharma:* "It is not a religion of chastity, it is a religion of selfishness. Fools do whatever you say as whatever manner you say, s/he agrees.so there is no question of not accepting it as meaning of this religion is exactly this — believe whatever your husband says. If he says, jump in the well, immediately jump. This is selfish, self-centric religion. They do whatever they feel like doing. Even after their death this religion makes you cry. They may rest next to the prostitute boys; but make us hear the glory and greatness of religion from Pandit ji."[197] What an attitude and argument — it is obvious that Hindi literary historians could not like it! In the case of Rukhma Bai (1864-1955) the male writers of Bhartendu era had stated their stand anyway. Most of the Hindi writers sided with Tilak, not

196 V.S.Mall (edit) Pratapnarayan-Granthāvalī, Nagari Pracharini Sabha, Varanasi, 1992, p.134

197 Seemantani Updesh, ibid, p.107

with Ranade, Bhandarkar or Gokhale.[198] No wonder that Hardevi did not get due importance. Hardly anyone has considered women writers or Hardevi while talking about the late nineteenth century Hindi literature. Countless histories of Hindi literature have been written, but difficult to find what Hardevi has written, what were her concerns, what issues she had raised? Only information that you may come across is that she was the editor of *Bharat Bhagini* as Dr. Ram Vilas Sharma has kindly recorded, "In the absence of female education, it was a dream for women to become writers, yet Shri Haridevi, the wife of a barrister from Prayag, Brought out a magazine named 'Bharat Bhagini' which was coming out till the time Radhakrishna Das wrote a book on Hindi characters. Shri Haridevi used to write in other journals like 'Bhartendu' etc. too and she was a good writer of her time."[199] Leaving aside the misspelling of the writer, the question remains that the critic has not described or given any details about her works, didn't even consider it necessary to name her works, why? Was Hardevi's writing so insignificant or this is the way to make women disappear from the history?

---

198 Nationalists like Bal Gangadhar Tilak considered appealing to the British to make laws to reform Hindu society as wrong, they saw it as external interference in the internal matter of Hinduism; hence when Rukhma Bai approached the court to annul her child marriage with her husband, Tilak opposed it. For details see,.Sudhir Chandra, *Enslaved Daughters Colonialism, Law and Women's Rights*, Oxford University Press, New Delhi, 2008.

199 Ramvilas Sharma, Bhartendu Yug, Vinod Pustak Mandir, Agra, 1956, p.29

9

Tender Women Voice: Anthologies of Hindi Poetesses in Pre-Independent India

There is a long tradition of compiling anthologies in India—- Rig-Veda[200] (c.1500 BCE) onwards hundreds of anthologies on various subjects and topics were conceived and executed in Sanskrit, Prakrit, Pali and later in other vernacular languages.[201] These anthologies including most of the Vedic corpus were compiled for distinct reasons with distinct objectives.[202] For example, Therigatha that is generally considered as "the first anthology of women's

200 *The form in which the samhita of the Rig-Veda has come down to us clearly shows that the different portions of the samhita represent chronologically different stages, follows from various indications of language, vocabulary, style, grammar, meter and lastly ideas."* V.S.Sukthankar, Ghate's lectures on Rigveda, Oriental Book Agency, Poona, Revised and enlarged second edition, 1926, p.58

201 *"Subhdsita-s are found in Sanskrit literature from the earliest times. Sententious verses already occur in the Rgveda, in great number in the Aitareya Brahmana, in the gatha-s in the Brahmana-s, in the Upanisad-s, in tbe epics and in the dharmas'astra-s. The oldest subhdsita-samgraha-s known to exist in India are Hala's Sattasai, Jayavallabha's Vajjalagga and the Chapannaya Gaha"* Ludwik Sternbach, Subhasita, Gnomic and Didactic Literature, Otto Harrassowitz, Wiesbaden 1974, p10

202 *"Though the Rig-Veda is much more natural in character than other samhitas and is not purely liturgical like others, still there are distinct traces of a deliberate arrangement and the influence of priests,...when we consider the divisions into which the samhita is divided."* V.S.Sukthankar, ibid, p.59

literature in the world"[203] is a part of Buddhist scripture. It is the ninth texts in the Khuddaka Nikāya,(Collection of Short Pieces or minor collection), the last collection of the Sutta Piṭaka in the Pāli Canon. Therīgāthā contains a total of 73 groups of poems in 522 stanzas and traditionally it is ascribed to certain theris (elder bhikhunis) of Buddha's time as mentioned in its commentary of Dhammpala's Paramatthdipani (5th century A.D.).[204] In this famous commentary not only the poems were discussed but the lives of poetess were also recorded.[205] Unfortunately this tradition of women centric compilation of anthology could not evolve in later years. Most of the post-Vedic Subhasita anthologies in Sanskrit were conceived as sublime utterances that should be preserved as a priceless storehouse for humanity. Vidyakar in the benedictory stanza of the oldest anthology in Sanskrit Subhasitaratnakosh[206]

203 Therigatha, Tr.Charles Haliisey, Murti Classical library of India, Harvard University Press, Cambridge, Massachusetts, 2015, p.vii

204 Therigatha or Pourings in verse of the Buddhist Bhikkhunis, N.K.Bhagwat(ed.), Bombay University Publications, 1956, p.ii

205 *Scholars consider it probable that these compositions, which were used by the itinerant theris as they wandered around preaching their message of release, were reworked over the five centuries in which they circulated orally. In the process the sound values, the images, the colour and detail in which feeling and situation were evoked would have been recast as the preachers responded to the requirements of the women they addressed. Obviously the biographical accounts would have gone through a similar dialogical process of refinement before they were collected and committed to writing in the fifth century* A.D. Women Writing in India, p.65

206 Vidyakara's Subhasitaratnakosh(1100-1130) is the first Sanskrit anthology among so many illustrious anthologies discovered later like Sad-ukti-karnamrta of Sridharadasa (1205), Suktimuktavali of Jalhana (1258), Sangadhar-paddhati (1363), Subhasitavali of Vallabhadeva (15th century) Prasannasahityaratnakara of Nandana (15th century), Vidagdhajanavallabha of Vallabhadeva, (15th century), Suktiratnahara of Surya and Subhasita-sudha-nidhi of Sayana (15th century), Padyavali of Rupa Goswami(End of

says: *I shall make up a priceless store/of charming words by sundry master poets, /such as have ornamented expert throats/and made great poets nod in approbation.*[207]Generally, these "*subhasita-samgraha-s* are divided according to the three or four *purusartha-s* and deal with *dharma, artha* and *kama* and in some cases also with *moksa.* The first Prakrit *subhasita-samgraha-s,* the Suktiratnahara, the Subhasita-sudha-nidhi and some Tamil anthologies (e.g. the Nalatiyar and theTiru-k-kural) are divided in this way. The division of Bhartrhari's epigrams and some collections of stray verses based on these epigrams is similar; these collections are divided into three parts—*niti {dharma* and *artha), vairagya {dharma* and *moksa)* and *sringara {Kama* and *artha).*[208]Although poems of women writers have been included in these anthologies[209] since long

the 15th, beginning of the16th century), Sringaralapa (1612) _Padyaracana of Laksmanabhatta Ankolakara (1625-1650) Rasikajivana of Gadadharabhatta (17th century) Subhasitaharavali of Harikavi (second half of the 17th century) Padyaveni of Venidatta (1644 or 1701) Suktisundara of Sundaradeva (1644-1701) Sabhyalankarana of Govindajit (after 1656) Padyamrta-tarangini of Haribhaskara (1674) Subhasita-sara-samuccaya (end of the 17th century) Subhasita-savaskrta (18th or 19th century) Vidyakara-sahasraka of Vidyakar Mishra(19th century).see, Ludwik Sternbach, A Descriptive Catalogue of Poets quoted in Sanskrit Anthologies and Inscriptions, Otto Harrassowitz, Wiesbaden, 1978, pp.3-4

207 An Anthology of Sanskrit Court Poetry, Vidyakar' s " Subhasitaratnakosh**,** *translated by* Daniel H. H. Ingalls,, Cambridge, Massachusetts, Harvard University Press, 1965, p.56

208 Ibid,, p.4

209 *Although it has not been possible to deal here with the innumerable poets of the Anthologies, a few words should/ be spared for the women-poets, who are chiefly, but inadequately, represented in the Anthologies. We have some 150 scattered verses of about 40 women-poets, of whom the names of Vijja, Vikatanitamba, Silabhattarika, Bhavadevi, Gauri, Padmavati and Vidyavati stand out*

from the time of Rig-Veda[210] but exclusive anthology of women writing like Therigatha was not conceived in Sanskrit ever. In vernacular languages women writing were continuously created and compiled albeit in non-women-centric anthologies all through the medieval period. Pre-Modern Poetesses like Meerabai, Sekh Rangrezan, Taj Bibi, Indu, Tara, Praveen Rai, Khaganiya were aptly compiled in famed Hindi Anthologies like *Kalidas Hazara*(ed. By Kalidas Trivedi, 1698), *Ragkalpdrum* (ed. by Krishnanand Vyas, 1843), *Digvijay Bhushan*(ed. By Lala Gokul Prasad, 1862), *Bhasha Kavya Sangraha*(ed. By Mahesh Dutt, 1873) *Kavitt Ratnakar*(ed. By Matadin Mishra, 1876) or Shivsingh Saroj (1877).It is only in the beginning of 20th century that exclusive anthology of women writings has started to come in the light. It all started with the publication of *Mahila Mriduvani* (1904), a poetry collection of thirty five Hindi women writers[211], edited by Munshi Devi Prasad 'Munshif' (1847-1923). In a short preface of the anthology he emphasized the fact that, *"Male alone has not been the treasure-*

---

prominently both in extent and variety of their verses

A History of Sanskrit Literature, VOL. I, S. N. Dasgupta and, S.K.De, Calcutta University Press, 1947, p.416

210 *As per the definition yasya vakyam sa rsi Brhaddevatakara Rsi Saunaka has presented twenty seven Rsikas in three slokas in Brhaddevata. Ghosa godha viswawara apalopanisannisat/brahmajaya jahurnama agastyasya/indrani cendramata ca sarama romasorvasi/lopamudra ca nadyasca yami nari ca sasvati/ srirlaksa sarparajni vak sraddha medha ca dakshina/ratri surya ca Savitri brahmavadinya iritah* /Rsikas of the Rgveda, Swamini Atmaprajnananda Saraswati, D K Printwortld Delhi, first published 2013, p.3

211 इस संग्रह में कविरानी चौबे, लोकनाथ जी, स्त्री अर्धांगिनी जी, ठाकुरानी काकरेची जी, कुशला, खगनिया, गिरिधर कविराय की स्त्री, चंद्रकला बाई, चाम्पादेरानी, छत्रकुंवरी बाई, जामसुता जाडेची जी, श्री प्रताप बा, झीमा, पंडितानी तीजांजी, ताज, तुलछराय, पद्मा, बीरा, प्रतापकुंवरी बाई, मीराबाई, बाघेली श्री रणछोड़ कुंवरी जी, महारानी जी श्री रत्न् कुंवरी बाई जी, रसिक बिहारी, रामप्रिया जी, रायप्रवीन या प्रवीनराय, बाघेली विष्णुप्रसाद कुंवर जी, बिरजूबाई, विरंजी कुंवर, बिहारी सतसई के कर्ता की स्त्री, बिहारीदास की पुत्री, ब्रजदासी, शेख रंगरेजन, श्री सरस्वती देवी, सहजोबाई, सुन्दर कुंवरीबाई, हरीजी रानी चावड़ी जी जैसी ३५ कवयित्रियों की रचनाएँ संकलित हैं।

house of all knowledge rather women too, at times, and still have been blessed with the divine attributes of intellectual knowledge and the art of poetry along with their usual ornaments of silver, gold and precious stones and their stories can still be found in many books and legends."[212] Munshi Devi Prasad, who was by profession a munsif magistrate, was also known for his history writing based on vernacular source materials[213]. In fact this anthology was byproduct of his quest to write a history of vernacular poets.[214]This anthology is remarkable on two counts: firstly it compiles a Therigatha –like exclusive anthology of women writing in Hindi for the first time and secondly its biographical sketches of poetesses has supplied enough material for literary historiography. It cannot be simply coincidence that after the publication of this anthology the most comprehensive source book of Hindi literary historiography, *Mishrabandhu Vinod* (1913) describes 89 women writers while earlier historians like Garcin de Tassy[215](1794 – 1878) mentions only seven women

---

212 "..अकेले पुरुष ही चौदह विद्यानिधान नहीं हुए हैं, वरन स्त्रियाँ भी समय -समय पर ऐसी होती रही हैं जो सोने -चांदी और रत्नजड़ित आभूषणों के अतिरिक्त विद्या -बुद्धि और काव्यकला के दिव्यभूषणों से भी भूषित थीं और अब भी हैं जिन के बखान अनेक पुस्तकों और जनश्रुतियों में विद्यमान हैं।" महिलामृदुवाणी, भूमिका, काशी नागरी प्रचारिणी सभा, बनारस, १९०५

213 *"The tradition of writing history, based on original source-material commenced by Tod, Shyamaldas, Suryamal Mishra during the 19th century, was continued with more vigorous efforts in the first half of the present century and Rajasthan produced a galaxy of historians like Ramnath Ratnu(1860-1902), Munshi Devi prasad(1847-1923), Ram Karan Asopa(1857-1945), Gauri Shankar Hirachand Ojha(1863-1947)..."*Cultural Contours of India, Vijayshankar Srivastava,(ed), Abhinav Publications, Delhi, p.42

214 "हमने जो भाषा कवियों का इतिहास लिखने के लिए प्राचीन ग्रंथों और कविवृत्तान्तों की खोज की थी तो उस प्रसंग में कुछ कविता ऐसी भी मिली जो काव्यकुशला कमलाओं के कोमल मुखारविंदों की निकली हुई थीं।हमने उसी को संग्रह करके यह छोटा -सा ग्रन्थ बनाया है और महिला मृदुवाणी नाम रखा है।" महिलामृदुवाणी, वही

215 'The Histoire de la littérature hindoue e hindoustani (1839, 1847) in French, which is considered to be the first literary history of Hindi mentions seven women writer: Karma Bai, Zana Begum, Meera Bai, Prema Bai, Mukta Bai, Ratnavali and Rupmati.

writers and, Shivsingh Sengar[216](1833-1878) and George Abraham Grierson[217](1851 – 1941) recounts only five poetess in their history.

This is worth noting that women questions were very much on the rise during first few decades of twentieth century.[218]In Hindi heartland women like Uma Nehru (1884-1963)[219], Rameshwari Nehru (1886-1966),[220] and Gopal Devi[221] were editing influential journals of their time and inspiring personalities

---

216 Shivsingh Saroj (1877) discusses five women writer—Praveen Rai Paturi, Praveen Kavirai, Premsakhi, Meera Bai, Ratnakunwari.

217 The modern vernacular literature of Hindustan' (1888) in Toto follows Shivsingh Saroj and discusses the same women author.

218 *"The nineteenth century was a period in which the rights and wrongs of women became major issues. If early attempts at reforming the condition under which Indian Women lived were largely conducted by men, by the late nineteenth century their wives, sisters, daughters, protégés and others affected by campaigns, such as that for women's education had themselves joined in movements. By the early twentieth century women's own autonomous organizations began to be formed and within a couple of decades by the thirties and forties, a special category of 'women's activism' was constructed."*Radha Kumar, The History of Doing, Zubaan, Delhi, First Published 1993

219 She was an active member of the famous Nehru family. She used to write frequently in *Stree Darpan*, in which she expressed feminist views, quite ahead of her time. She fiercely critiqued Miss Mayo' Mother India' in her book *Mother India Aur Uska Jawab*, in 1928. She took part in the Salt March and the Quit India Movement and was subsequently imprisoned. After the independence, she was twice elected to the Lok Sabha and from 1962 until her death; she was a member of the Rajya Sabha.

220 She too was a member of Nehru family(she was married to Brijlal Nehru, a nephew of Motilal Nehru) She was a poet, writer who edited *Stri Darpan*, from 1909 to 1924.She was the president of women's committee of the Indian League, 1931-33 and also one of the founders of All India Women's Conference (AIWC) and was elected its president in 1942.

221 Gopaldevi was editing *Grihlakshmi* with her husband Sudarshan Acharya, one of the most popular periodicals of her time.

like Srimati Hardevi (c.1863- 1926)[222], Hemant Kumari Devi (1868-1953)[223] Rajrani Devi (1870-1928)[224], Bundela Bala (1883-1909), Chandravati Lakhanpal, (1904-1969)[225] Shubhadra Kumari Chauhan (1904-48) and Mahadevi Verma (1907-87) were also articulating consciously their distinct experiences for the praxis of change in the society. It is being said that, "The women's movement in the Hindi provinces around the time of world war I is significantly different from the nineteenth century reform movements, in the fact that it was led by women, and in that it raised questions from the standpoint of women rather than that of men."[226] What was termed as 'The Age of Periodicals' (1900-1920)[227] was replete with women's journals and that were full of women issues. Exclusive

222 Srimati Hardevi, a child widow herself was an educationist, social reformer, a regular member of National Social Conference and a true revolutionary as She condemned two taboos—widow remarriage and seafaring in her own life. considered to be the first women editor (editor of *Bharat Bhagini*:1889) and author of travelogue like *landon yatra*,(1888) *landon Jubilee*(1889) and novel like *Hukmdevi:Hindu Dharma ki Uchchata me ek sachchi Kahani*(1892) and so many social reformative tracts like simantani updesh, and .

223 Hemant Kumari Devi was daughter of famous educationist and Brahmo Samaji Navin Chandra Rai. She is considered to be the first women journalist in Hindi, the editor of journal for women- *Sugrihini* (1888).

224 Rajrani Devi was one of the earliest practioners of khari Boli in Hindi poetry and content -wise her poetry was quite ahead of most of the poets of Bhartendu Circle.

225 Chandravati Lakhanpal social reformer written four books in Hindi,:*Mother India ka Jawab(1924)*, Striyon ki Sthiti(1934), shiksha manovigyaan(1934) and shiksha shastra (co-authored with her husband Satyavrat Sidhantalankar) she became Member of Parliament after independence for ten years(1952-62)

226 Vir Bharat Talwar, Feminist Consciousness in Women's Journals in Hindi, 1910-20 in Recasting Women, Kumkum Sangari, Suresh Vaid, (ed.) Kali for Women, New Delhi, Reprint 1993, p.206

227 The Rise and Growth of Hindi Journalism, Ram Ratan Bhatnagar, Kitab Mahal, Allahabad, 1947, p.ix

women's Journals like *Grihlakshmi* (1909), *Stree Darpan* (1909), *Kumari Darpan*(1916), *Arya Mahila*(1917), *Chand* (1922) all published from Allahabad except Arya Mahila that must have raised the consciousness of the city(if not the whole nation!), so much so that three consecutive anthologies of women writing were compiled there. *Stri-Kavi-Kaumudi* (1931), edited by Jyoti Prasad Mishra 'Nirmal', *Hindi Kavya ki kokilayein*(1933), edited by Girija Dutt Shukla and *Hindi Kavya Ki kalamayee Tarikayen*(1941) edited by Vyathit Hridaya, all published from Allahabad have established the trend emphatically what *Mahila Mriduvani* had initiated with a patronizing gesture.

The art of Anthology does not mean merely collecting materials but compiling materials with a purpose and that purpose is the key to understand compiler's temperament vis. a vis. the temperament of the age. Pre-Independent India of twentieth century can be termed as one of the most turbulent period of Indian history, society was churning, so its values, its mores, its history, its cultural practices, everything was being questioned and of course women question was also hotly debated issue. In such a scenario, is it possible to treat these anthologies, the way some scholars studied women's periodicals as 'disseminators of ideologies?'[228]

Stri-Kavi-Kaumudi contains thirty nine poetesses in which nineteen poetess were repeated from *Mahila Mriduvani* and it also contains a section called *'Kusum-Mala'* in which one poem each of forty contemporary poetess were collected. In his 'statement' of *Stri-Kavi-Kaumudi* Jyoti Prasad Mishra 'Nirmal' boldly equated women

228 *"Periodicals may thus be read as disseminators of ideologies pertaining to women's role in public and private. They may be understood as part of yet another discursive formation of womanhood, this time with women as driving force."*Shobhana Nijhawan, Women and Girls in the Hindi Public Sphere: Periodical Literature in Colonial North India, Oxford University Press, First Published 2012

writers with coetaneous canonical male writers: "If Tulsi, Bihari, Dev and Padmakar are considered as savior of ancient literature than Mirabai, Sahjobai, Dayabai aur Sundarkunwari Bai had done no less ...if Surdas has composed lovely songs of Krishna devotion so does Mirabai...if Bihari, Dev.Padmakar and Gwal is renowned for their erotic compositions so do Sekh, Pravinrai, Champade and especially, Sekh's compositions are second to none...The way Poets like Giridhar Kavirai, Vrind have shown their spectacle skill of writing didactic poetry, exactly the same way poetesses like Sai, Chatrakunwari Bai and others have been successful to enrich the storehouse of Hindi with equally beautiful didactic poems... In the field of riddles (Samasya-Purti) Dwijbaldev, Pandit Nathuram Shankar Sharma, Ambika Dutt Vyas, Rai Devi Prasad 'Purna' etc. has made their name.Chandrakala Bai of Bundi too had made good name of herself by composing and solving beautiful riddles —smt.Toran Devi Shukla 'Lali, smt.Rama Devi, Bundela Bala too became famous in this area...when Khari Boli has replaced Braj Bhasha, poets like Pandit Nathuram Shankar Sharma, Snehi, Pandit Ayodhyasingh Upadhyay, Rai Devi Prasad'Purn' started writing poetry in Khari Boli... Poetess like Smt.Toran Devi Shukla 'Lali', Smt. Rama Devi, Bundela Bala too were writing in Khari Boli...when Chayavad and Mysticism emerged, Sri Sumitranandan Pant, Sri Jaishankar 'Prasad' and Sri Nirala led the way ...the name of Smt. Mahadevi Verma, in this regard is also notable... The nation is marching ahead for independence and many poets have produced national literature by writing patriotic songs to awaken the society. Sri Snehi, pandit Madhav Shukla, Shankar ji, Harioudh Ji has written successful patriotic poems, likewise Bundelabala, Sriraj Devi, Srimati Toran Devi Shukla 'Lali' and Shubhadrakumari Chauhan has composed very beautiful patriotic songs —that's why their name along with male poets generate so much respect."[229]This new assertion of equality is noteworthy but unfortunately the long article of Ramshankar Shukla 'Rasal' in this anthology neutralizes it to a great extent. The fifty eight page long article titled 'Women Writing in Hindi: Historical Evolution' apparently takes a patronizing gesture towards women writing but mostly underrates it. In one place evaluating Meera, he opines, "if we look at the sensibilities of the Meera's poetry we find full reflection of the sensibilities of our great male poets like Kabir, Surdas, Tulsi, Dev and Jayasi and on that count Meera is comparable with them although Meera has neither the equal sublime sensibility nor the poetic skill nor the perfection of language as these great masters possess."[230]Equally disdainful is his evaluation of Sekh, when he speculates, "Sekh's poetry seems as if it is created by some good poet. We find in it the fantabulous speeches, uncanny depths, elegance of language and skill for artistic poetry in good measures. This is the reason I guess it is Alam's creation who has given Sekh's name on it to make her immortal."[231] This is a good example to illustrate how gender makes you biased. But to be fair with him, it must be added that he is very sympathetic, when he evaluates poetesses like Rani Bankavati 'Brajdasi", Sundarkunwari Bai, Pratap kunwari Bai, Ratnakunwari Bai, Bagheli vishnuprasad kunwari who belongs to, if we use his nomenclature 'Queen-poet-class'. [232] In fact, the ambivalence that existed towards women in the society has been expressed in the opposing views of Jyoti Prasad Mishra 'Nirmal' and Ramshankar Shukla 'Rasal'.

---

229 Stree-Kavi-Kaumudee, Jyoti Prasad Mishra 'Nirmal',(ed.), Gandhi Hindi Pustak Bhandar, Prayag, March 1931, pp. 11-15

230 Ibid, p.50

231 Ibid, p.52

232 See, Ibid, pp.26-29

This was the time of Cultural nationalism[233] in India and conserving the indigenous cultural traditions was on the rise. Poems collected in *Stri-Kavi-Kaumudi* tries its best not only to collect traditional poetry but also compiles contemporary new voices of resistance too. Poetess like Bundela Bala, Raj Devi, Toran Devi Shukla 'Lali' Priyamvada Devi, Shubhadra Kumari Chauhan broke the boundary of so called traditional subject-matter for women writing and depicted their version of truth regarding colonialism, nationality, family and so on and so forth. Bundela Bala, in her poem 'Dialogue between mother and son'[234], mother introduces the geography of India with its cultural contours to her son in such a way that he may be proud to be an Indian. Likewise in another poem (we need such sons) she discusses what type of child we need.[235]Gopal Devi, the editor of famous 'Grihlakshmi' describes in one of her poems that Ayurveda should be known to everyone so people could know the healthy way of living and mother can diagnose the disease of her own son.[236] Raj Devi, the elder sister of famous Shubhadra Kumari Chauhan has written some poems like Desh ki Durdasha(*Plight of the Country),* Prachin

233 *"Cultural nationalism generally refers to ideas and practices that relate to the intended revival of a purported national community's culture. If political nationalism is focused on the achievement of political autonomy, cultural nationalism is focused on the cultivation of a nation. Here the vision of the nation is not a political organization, but a moral community. As such, cultural nationalism sets out to provide a vision of the nation's identity, history and destiny. The key agents of cultural nationalism are intellectuals and artists, who seek to convey their vision of the nation to the wider community."* Eric Taylor Woods, (https://stateofnationalism.eu/article/cultural-nationalism/ accessed on 9.7.2018)

234 Ibid, p.256

235 Ibid, p.249

236 Ibid, p.260

Gaurav (*Ancient Glory*) in a scathing manner that was till then, not common, especially in women writers. Most of the poems of Toran Devi Shukla 'Lali' deal with patriotic idealism —-poems like *karmabhumi, jai Swadesh, Sadhusilata* out rightly aim to awaken her countryman. Medieval poetess from Meera onwards has always fancied themselves as gopi or Radha while addressing Krishna but Shubhadra Kumari Chauhan sends Rakhi to Him for rescuing India from the oppression of colonial masters in her poem *Rakhi*[237]. Her iconic poem *Jhansi ki Rani,* is a saga of feminine courage and brevity and its treatment of 1857, the first war of independence is truly inspirational and exceptional in Hindi. The last poetess of this anthology is Mahadevi Verma, who is also considered to be the last poet of a literary movement called *Chayavad (1918-36),* a kind of Romanticism in Hindi. Other than its new awareness about nature and ecology this literary movement expressed the ongoing cultural nationalism in most sophisticated language and form. It was quite a departure from the earlier phase (Dwevedi Yug: 1900-1918) and it can be testified comparing Mahadevi's poems from the poems of others in this anthology. Although this anthology was prepared during the high time of Chayavad, its impact on this anthology seems meager. The straightforward narrative and its matter of fact style of presentation with the use of language as merely communicating tool (the hallmark of Dwevedi-period) is antithetical to subjective perception, sweep of imagination, metaphorical style of Chayavad where language was treated as distinct means of individual expression.

After two years of the publication of *Stree-Kavi-Kaumudi*, another anthology on women writing, *Hindi Kavya Ki Kokilayein* (Cuckoos of Hindi Poetry) edited by Girijadutt Shukla and

237 Ibid, p.345

Brajbhushan Shukla was brought out by Sahitya-Mandir, Prayag. This anthology is divided in three parts —first part contains Braj Bhasha poems of sixteen poetesses from Meera to Saraswati Devi, Khari Boli poems are compiled in second (six poetess, from Rajrani Devi to Shubhadra Kumari Chauhan) and third part (Nine poetesses from Mahadevi Verma to Lilawati Jhanwar 'Satya'. Compared to *Stree-Kavi-Kaumodi* its analytical part is more elaborate and provocative. It is also interesting to observe the evolution of those poetesses in this anthology, who were compiled in *Stree-Kavi-Kaumodi* as budding poetess like Purusharthavati Devi,(1911-1931), Rameshwari Devi Goyal(1911-), Rameshwari Devi Mishra Chakori(1915-), Rajrajeswari Devi 'Nalini', Taradevi Pandey, and Lilawati Jhanwar 'Satya', but now became matured enough to get independent treatment. The impact of Chayavad and especially of Mahadevi Verma on their poetry is very much evident and to some extent it can be said about the whole part one and part two of this anthology[238].

This anthology, though claims to be 'critical' but gives no reference to any earlier anthologies, in general followed the format of *Stree-Kavi-Kaumudi* with some minor differences.[239] The main difference lies in its editor(s)'s tone of moral guardianship and an

---

238 It is not true what Suman Raje asserts that most of the contemporary of Mahadevi are not influenced by her poetry; rather its opposite is true. See, Hindi Sahitya ka Aadha Itihas, Bhartiya Gyanpith, Delhi, Third edition 2006, p.256

239 'Even all collected poetess are repeated from *Stree-Kavi-Kaumudi* with only one exception of Vishnu Kumari Srivastava'Manju.' There are thirty one main poetesses in this anthology and five miscellaneous in which thirty are repeated from *Stree-Kavi-Kaumudi*, twenty four from main list and six from 'Kusum-mala' and its miscellany 'Awshesh'contains five poetess in which one poetess is repeated from the earlier anthology.

ambition of becoming torchbearer for budding writers. In one place, editor-duo opines, "*The question is, artistic image of which ideal these women are going to impart in their art of poetry? What type of men and women are their words going to create for activating our inner hidden creative powers? Can poetry of Sekh or Pravinrai guide our women? Answer is simply 'No'. Whatever art we find in them that may have some power to lure human heart but there is no capability to develop one's personality." 'To whom we should follow?' if it is asked to us, our reply would be to follow the footsteps of Meera and if they don't carry Meera's prowess then they should try to follow the path shown by Sripratap Kunwari, Srigiriraj Kunwari, Srirajarani Devi, Srimati Shubhadra Kumari Chauhan or Mahadevi Verma."* [240]*The compilers have a ready prescription for writing good poetry and they do not hesitate to instruct whenever needed, for example, observing flamboyance in Rameshwari Devi Mishra 'Chakori', they advised her 'to restrain in expressing her innermost feelings of the heart'*[241]Similarly after quoting Mahadevi Verma where she confessed that suffering and pain in her poetry is not reflection of her personal life since she got enough affection, respect and everything in life; editor-duo commented that, "*when there is no truth in one's own pain then he/she can never sympathize with his/her neighbour and in that situation it is absurd to expect in their writing the pain and suffering of his/her nation.*"[242]

The last anthology on women poetry in Pre-independent India appeared in 1941; titled *Hindi Kavya ki Kalamayee Tarikayen,* it was edited by Sri Vyathit Hridaya with a preface of Ramshankar Shukla 'Rasal', which says, "*Beautiful Poetry from Meera to major poetesses*

240 Hindi Kavya ki Kokilayen, Girijadutt Shukla, Brajbhushan Shukla(eds.), Sahitya-Mandir, Prayag, 1933, p.285

241 Ibid, p.219

242 Ibid, p.175

of present times are compiled in this anthology by a clever critic and an able compiler, who has heart of a poet. Although anthologies like Stree-Kavi-Kaumudi by Sri Nirmal ji and similar books by other writers had already been published before, but critical parts in them were lacking which is being tried to fulfill in this anthology."[243]This anthology contains thirty eight poetesses, in which twenty seven were repeated from *Hindi Kavya Ki Kokilayein* and like earlier anthologies there is also one section of budding poetesses in which twelve authors are compiled.

The importance of this anthology doesn't lies in its critical evaluation of compiled poetry, as its preface claims but its ability to introduce some new faces like Ramkumari Chauhan, Mangla Balupuri, Sawitri Devi, Homvati Devi, Suryadevi Dikshit 'Usha', Shakuntala Devi Kare, Hiradevi Chaturvedi, Kumari Vidya Bhargava etc. But it is astonishing to see that majority of the poems do not reflect any change of sensibility or forms, what was observed in Hindi literary history with the emergence of *Pragativad* (Progressivism).It was still the same sensibility, same diction, same imagery, same trope popularized by Chayavad, what they were practicing. In short, this anthology may be considered passable.

In conclusion, it can be said that these anthologies, that are not edited by women neither its editorial preface emphasizes any feminist agenda but this very idea to present women writers in such exclusive collections in itself is praiseworthy. It is also true that under the influence of cultural nationalism, these anthologies were intended to emphasize the wealth of women writing in India and at times, also patronizing in its treatment but it never fails, not

243 Hindi Kavya ki Kalamayee Tarikayen, Sri Vyathit Hridaya (ed), Pramod Pustak Mala, Katara, Prayag, Jan1941, p.5

always consciously, to reveal the beauty and shortcomings of Hindi women writing in its historical context. They are, in some sense symptomatic and at the same time byproduct of the discursive Hindi public sphere of pre-independent India. Although, in some other context, as we know "*The arguments against anthologies are familiar and obvious. Instead of an intense intimate friendship with the choicest flowers in the garden of literature, it is felt that they give us the bird's-eye view from the far-off airship that takes in everything and penetrates nothing. Or perhaps the reader may be compared to a traveler in an express train, rushing through provinces but never knowing a personality. Books of selections, it is argued, are scrappy and superficial.*"[244]But undoubtedly it serves different purpose in a situation where flowers in the garden of literature are yet to become countless or innumerable to choose from; so choices are limited but intimacy with them consequently becomes more natural and compulsive, and in that way its selection ceases to become 'scrappy and superficial'.

244 The Use of Anthology in the Study of Literature, Philip H. Churchman, The Modern Language Journal, Vol. 7, No. 3 (Dec., 1922), pp. 149-154

10

Modernity in Hindi Literature: Indigenous, Colonial or Global?

It is a generally believed notion that the process of modernization usually leads to modernity but it is a hotly debatable issue that when and where this process started in India—-in Mughal India or in British India so consequently as argument goes, the modernity developed in India is indigenous in character or Colonial or modernity should simply be discussed as an universal category. If we define modernity as universal category and accordingly judge our society, it is possible to term it as "mistaken modernity." as one of our modern sociologists Dipankar Gupta has concluded, "Modernity has been misrecognised in India because of the tendency to equate it with technology and with other contemporary artefacts.The possession of modern technology, however, does not always signal modernity. Modernity has to do with attitudes, especially those that come into play in social relations. A modern society is one in which at least the following characteristics must be present: Dignity of the individual; Adherence to universalistic norms; Elevation of individual achievement over privileges or disprivileges of birth; Accountability in public life. Once these attributes are in place, it does not really matter if there is high level technology, superfast transit systems, or consumerism. Generally speaking, technology and consumerism are consequences of the four characteristics of modernization listed above, and do not by themselves constitute modernity."[245]But as we know now that modernity or modernization is not either a homogenous process or confined to single time and space[246]. Sudipta Kaviraj has rightly pointed out that, "Theorists who analyze modern European history acknowledge that the phenomenon called modernity is not a single, homogeneous process, but a combination of several which can be isolated and distinguished. When we are talking about modernity, we are talking about a number of processes of social change which can be studied or analyzed independently of each other such as, capitalist industrialization, the increasing centrality of the state in the social order (Foucault's "governmentality'), urbanization, sociological individuation, secularization in politics and ethics, the creation of a new order of knowledge, vast changes in the organization of family and intimacy, and changes in the fields of artistic and literary culture."[247]Here, in this paper the changes in the field of Hindi literary culture will be discussed.

---

245 Dipankar Gupta, Mistaken Modernity, Harper Collins Publishers India, Eight impression 2016, pp.12-13

246 "Modernity in the West thus alludes to two separate projects that are symbiotically connected. One refers to processes of building the institutions (from parliamentary and legal institution to roads, capitalist businesses, and factories) that are invoked when we speak of modernization. The other refers to the development of a degree of reflective, judgmental thinking about these processes. The latter is what is often invoked by the term "modernity." The distinction is, of course, only analytical; for the development of ideas and the development of institutions are in reality inter twined processes." Dipesh Chakravarty, *The Muddle of Modernity*, The American Historical Review, Vol. 116, No. 3 (June 2011), pp. 663-675, Oxford University Press on behalf of the American Historical Association

247 Sudipta Kaviraj, *An Outline of a Revisionist Theory of Modernity*, European Journal of Sociology, Volume 46, Issue 03, December 2005, p.508

Let us start with Hindi Fiction. The rise of Novel is a modern phenomenonandinMilanKundera'swordsitis"Europe'screation'.[248] Granted but in our context, the most pertinent question would be, when it came to India whether it was grafted on some live and long tradition of fiction here or it was consumed as it was?. Vasudha Dalmia writes, "The emergence of the novel in India has had a symbiotic relationship with its own modernity. Individual novels both anticipated and documented a host of cultural and social changes in Indian society in what can roughly be named a modernizing era from at least the 19th century onwards.Yet, there is still some uncertainty about what was entirely "new" about the form itself. Did the literary production that was ushered in, by and in opposition to the colonial presence, signify a rupture with past traditions? Must the emergence of the novel be seen as a radical break with the literary modes preceding it?"[249]so these questions lead to the binaries of modernity in India, namely, continuity and rupture in tradition or Tradition and Modernity as a whole. If we survey the Hindi literary production of late nineteenth century to forties of twentieth century, novel from *Parikshaguru* (The Tutelage of Trials, Lala Srinivas Das, 1882) to *Sekhar: Ek Jeevani*(Ajneya, Sekhar:A Life:1940) Poetry from *Jagat-sachchai-saar* (Sridhar Pathak, Essence of world-truth:1887) to *Taar-Saptak*(Ajneya, ed.1943), Drama from *Andher-Nagri*(Bhartendu, Dark-City:1881) to *Dhruvswamini(*Jaishankar Prasad, 1933), Criticism from *Natak*(Bhartendu, Drama:1883) to *Trishanku* (Ajneya, 1945) it is evident that our writers never perceived tradition as anti-thesis to modernity. Not only in their theoretical deliberations on drama

---

248 Milan Kundera, *The Art of Novel*, Faber and Faber, London Boston, 1988, p.6

249 Vasudha Dalmia, *Merchant Tales and the Emergence of the Novel in Hindi*, Economic and Political Weekly, Vol. 43, No. 34 (Aug. 23 - 29, 2008), p. 43,

but their plays itself are testimony of the fact that Bhartendu Harishchandra(1850-1885) and Jaishankar Prasad(1889-1937) both were equally conscious of the fact that how to make choices between our rasa theory and conflict ridden actions of the western modern plays. In fact, it was a constant search for finding a viable option by evaluating old methods of tradition with new ones introduced under colonialism simultaneously. Satya P. Mohanty also articulates it contextualizing Fakir Mohan Senapati in these words, "...colonialist ideological opposition between native tradition and western modernity was challenged forcefully by several nineteenth century writers in their literary creations—prose sketches, novels, and plays, for instance. While many Indian writers of the period implicitly accepted the ideology of "colonial modernity", others, as is evident in Senapati's novel, provided a more complex defence of what we may call the "rationality" of some traditional Indian social institutions. Modernity is thus a layered and complex phenomenon, according to such writers as Senapati, and analysis of traditional culture needs to be nuanced and contextually sensitive. These writers in effect prise apart the many layers of modernity in order to analyze them critically. Instead of identifying modernity with what colonial rule brought with it— and choosing to either accept it in its entirety or reject it outright —many in the colonized world defined modernity for their times through their complexly mediated critiques of their own social traditions, both the old and the newly invented ones."[250]

If we survey the Hindi fiction of nineteenth and early twentieth century it provides a counter-narrative of the 'cultural amnesia' what Velcheru Narayana Rao says of the babus and the upper castes of

250 Satya P. Mohanty(ed), *Colonialism Modernity and Literature*, orient black Swan Delhi, p.3

colonial India who, under influence of the new education, "rejected their immediate past in favour of colonial modernity."[251] But during late thirties and all through forties of twentieth century, especially works like Chitralekha (Bhagvati Charan Verma, 1934), Sunita (Jainendra Kumar, 1936), Tyagpatra(Jainendra Kumar, 1937), Sekhar: Ek Jeevani(Ajneya, 1940 & 1944) mark the beginning of an era, where interiority often replaced the social world as subject and the representation of the subjective consciousness of one or more characters with no external commentary, what is considered to be perhaps the most immediately distinguishing technique of the modernist novels with Stream of consciousness and a kind of Psychological realism[252] is very much evident. This phase can be termed as "spiritual", the way Virginia Woolf (1882-1941) has demarcated modern novels of James Joyce from the "materialist" novels of H.G.Wells (1866-1946), Arnold Bennett (1867-1931) and

---

251 Though Narayana Rao has argued on the basis of pre-colonial Telugu, Tamil, and Kannada literature but it is equally applicable for Hindi literature too that these literatures reveal a strong tradition of modernity in pre-colonial Indian culture, one that has been eclipsed by the assumption that British rule brought modernity to India. Focusing on Apparao's famous 1890s play Kanyasulkam (Girls for Sale) and Senapati's novel 'chha man aath guntha', he shows how both writers provide a counter to the "cultural amnesia" of the babus and the upper castes of colonial India who, under influence of the new education, "rejected their immediate past in favour of colonial modernity." and they were the one who later hailed as harbinger of the so called Indian Renaissance. Narayana Rao goes on to distinguish from this tendency the more complex critical approach of Senapati and Apparao, which he defines as an indigenous and non-colonialist strand of modernity. It can be argued that from Kabir to Lala Srinivas Das to Premchand this indigenous modernity is evident in Hindi too. see, Satya P. Mohanty(ed), ibid, p.136

252 Deborah Parsons, *Theorists of the Modernist Novel*, Routledge, London and New York, First Indian Reprint, 2015, p 56

John Galsworthy (1867-1931).[253] If we consider Peter J. Leithart's distinction of two modernities, the modernity of the Renaissance, and the modernity of the counter-Renaissance that is associated with the Enlightenment.[254]then this phase and especially Ajneya's work can be categorized in second category. Sekhar, the protagonist of the novel in Sekhar: Ek Jeevani", doubts and questions everything including traditional and contemporary value-system in true enlightened fashion with a kind of impersonality and self-reflexivity and these are the attributes what is considered to be the hallmark of a modern man. In this regard the insight of Sudipta Kaviraj is worth mentioning, he says, "In modern cultures people turn their capacity for rational reasoning and criticism upon themselves at least in two ways. Reflexivity leads to assessments of their own conduct from an *exterior* point of view, which was unavailable to non-European societies before the arrival of Western ideas. New influences broke the obviousness and the immovability of cultural habitus, the impossibility of conceiving the world in any except an "internal" way. This made it possible for non-Europeans to evaluate their own societies from a kind of Archimedean point, leading to rejection of conventional ways of social behaviour. Reflexivity however cannot stop there, simply using Western modernity as an exterior point of view that comprehensively undermines traditional cultures. The capacity for critical reflection extends to assessments of institutions and practices of Western modernity as well…"[255]

---

253 Virginia Woolf, Modern Fiction in McNeille, Andrew, Ed. *The Essays of Virginia Woolf. Volume 4: 1925 to 1928.*, The Hogarth Press, London, 1984.p.161

254 https://www.firstthings.com/blogs/leithart/2005/05/renaissance-and-modernity

255 Sudipta Kaviraj, Ibid, p.523

One good example for our attitude towards tradition as well as western modernity would be to see how a canonical text of Modernity like T.S.Eliot's (1888–1965) *'Tradition and Individual Talent'* (1919) was translated in Hindi."Roorhi aur Maulikata" (Tradition and Originality), is a free translation in Hindi of this classic essay by Sachchidananda Hirananda Vatsyayan 'Ajneya' (1911-1987). Original essay has this opening paragraph:

In English writing we seldom speak of tradition, though we occasionally apply its name in deploring its absence. We cannot refer to "the tradition" or to "a tradition"; at most, we employ the adjective in saying that the poetry of So-and-so is "traditional" or even "too traditional." Seldom, perhaps, does the word appear except in a phrase of censure. If otherwise, it is vaguely approbative, with the implication, as to the work approved, of some pleasing archeological reconstruction. You can hardly make the word agreeable to English ears without this comfortable reference to the reassuring science of archeology[256]

Hindi Translation starts with a quotation of T.S.Eliot's in original English (The more perfect the artist, the more completely separate in him will be the man who suffers and the mind which creates) and then it goes on like this: *"Indians are traditionalists" is a statement that we have all heard from time to time. Often we accept this to be true as well. There was once in such a statement a sense of admiration—it was thought to be a virtue of Indians that they abide by traditions; but today when there is so much talk of "progress," traditions have come to grace the role of the villain in the drama of our life . ... In literature too, the role of the villain in the drama of our life. ... In literature too, especially in the matter of criticism, it has become fashionable to hold tradition in contempt. . . . For example, we*

256 T.S.Eliot, *The sacred wood*, Faber and Faber, London p.47

often say that Hariaudh is a traditionalist, while Pant and Nirala are modernists, i.e., they are rebels against traditions."[257] Later he brings in part two of the essay, the concept of sthai bhava, sanchari bhava of Rasa theory to delineate the role of emotions and feelings in art and concludes by saying that essence (rasa) of art is gettable in art only and this experience cannot be compared with any other experience outside of it. In this regard, Harish Trivedi rightly pointed out that, "Ajneya's version is something more complex than a mere translation however free...Eliot's classic essay here is not a finished, received document to which Ajneya must show translatorial allegiance, but more like an agenda for discussion, a lump of clay out of which Ajneya will fashion something to his own critical liking and for his own creative use ...Clearly, this is no longer the essay Eliot wrote in 1919 to fashion an aesthetic principle out of his peculiar understanding of his European tradition in order to answer his own artistic needs. In Ajneya's hands, this essay is made to answer a similar need but in a later, local context which could hardly be more different, for Ajneya uses some of the arguments and selected strategies of this essay in order to render them relevant and helpful for the young Hindi poet of the 1940s. In this close and searching encounter, there is acceptance on Ajneya's part as well as rejection, receptivity as well as resistance, and a sense of the distantly alien no less than an eagerness to assimilate."[258] I think, this was the strategy most of our modernist writers adopted for not becoming the consumer of the global modernity but creator of our own. Partha Chatterjee is right when he emphasizes that, "... the way in which the history of our modernity has been intertwined

257 Translated from Hindi by Harish Trivedi, *Eliot in Hindi Modes of Reception*, Indian Literature, Vol. 32, No. 5 (133) (September-October, 1989), p.150

258 Ibid, pp.150-151

with the history of colonialism, we have never quite been able to believe that there exists a universal domain of free discourse, unfettered by differences of race or nationality. Somehow, from the very beginning, we have made a shrewd guess that given the close complicity between modern knowledges and modern regimes of power, we would forever remain consumers of universal modernity; never would we be taken seriously as its producers. It is for this reason that we have tried, for over a hundred years, to take our eyes away from this chimera of universal modernity and clear a space where we might become the creators of our own modernity."[259]

If we became creators of our own modernity, Credits must go, to some extent to our literature too.

---

259 Partha Chatterjee, *Empire & Nation*, Permanent Black, Ranikhet, First Paperback Edition 2012, p146

11

Women Writing and Hindi Renaissance

Two streams of social reform and nationalism are visible in the Indian Renaissance. Issues related to women—whether it is the question of women's education or sati, widow remarriage or mismatched marriages, polygamy, were included with utmost prominence in the projects of social reform. In that era, traditional values and conventions were debated and re-explored keeping women issues at the center[260]. Seeing this centrality of the women's question in the social sphere, if the nineteenth century is considered as the 'age of women', then it is not inappropriate[261]. It is believed that the stream of nationalism was strong in the Hindi Renaissance, but the trend of social reform has been very weak in comparison to Bengal, Maharashtra or the South India[262]. It is not surprising that the concept of Hindi Renaissance was formulated

260 "Tradition was thus not the ground on which the status of women was being contested. Rather the reverse was true: woman in fact became the site on which tradition was debated and reformulated." Lata Mani, *Contentious Tradition* in *Recasting Women*, Kumkum Sangari, Suresh Vaid,(eds.), Kali for Women, New Delhi, Reprinted 1993, p.118

261 The nineteenth century could well be called an age of women, for all over world their rights and wrongs, their 'nature', capacities and potential were the subjects of heated discussion. Radha Kumar, The History of Doing, Zubaan:Kali for Women, Delhi, Eigth Impression 2006, p.7

262 Vishalakshi Menon, Indian Women and Nationalism, The UP Story, Shakti Books, New Delhi, 2003, p.14

keeping the great narratives of feudalism, imperialism and anti-colonialism at the center[263]. It is true that there were differences of opinion everywhere on the question of setting priority between social reform and political independence, but the Hindi region, in the words of Nehru, was more afflicted by the 'disease of nationalism'[264].

Mahadev Govind Ranade (1842-1901) and Raghunath Rao (1831-1912), With the intention of giving sufficient attention to social matters parallel to political issues, in 1887, established the National Social Conference separately from the Indian National Congress. On reading the annual reports of the National Social Conference, it becomes clear that in those days, the issues and questions related to women were at the center of social reform. In the

263 For example, Dr. Ram Vilas Sharma, who introduced the concept of Hindi Renaissance emphasizes that: "India's national renaissance is generally associated with Raja Ram Mohan Roy. It may be true for Bengal. It is not necessary that the same process occurs in every state. Dwivedi ji was strongly opposed to making English the medium of education. He was a supporter of rationalism and scientific method of thinking and was against mysticism. He was in favor of industrialization of India. He was not convinced that the Indian economy should be formed in the old way on the basis of spinning wheel and loom. From the study of his writings, it is known that Hindi renaissance has its own characteristics; it is different from the renaissance of Bengal or Gujarat. These characteristics are also found in the Bhartendu era. ...In this way, the renaissance that began with the freedom struggle of 1857, became even more widespread in the Bhartendu era, its anti-imperialist, anti-feudal tendencies became stronger in the Dwivedi era." (Mahavir Prasad Dwivedi aur Hindi Navjagran, Rajkamal Prakashan Delhi, First Edition, 1977, Page 18-19)

264 "We suffer from the disease of nationalism, and that absorbs our attention and it will continue to do so till we get political freedom. Jawaharlal Nehru, An Autobiography, Oxford University Press, New Delhi, Fifth Impression, 1987, p.383

sixth National Social Conference of 1892, editor of *Bharat Bhagini* Smt. Hardevi (1859-1926), emphasized that the National Social Conference is more important than the Indian National Congress as "by the Indian National Congress the people hoped to get justice from the government. By the National Social Conference, they battered their social conditions. The justice which people expected at the hands of British government, ought to dispose them to do justice to those whose happiness and misery, joy and sorrow were intermixed with those of theirs. It is well said: "The Women's cause is man's / They rise or sink together, /Dwarfed, or god-like, bond or free."[265] By quoting this poem of Tennyson, Hardevi was making her point quite clear as she was one of the few women intellectuals in the male-dominated society of North India who tried to improve the condition of widows and women's education in the late nineteenth and early decades of the twentieth century but the details of which are not recorded anywhere in the historiography of modern India, Hindi literary history and propounder of Hindi renaissance also did not consider it appropriate to take cognizance of it, whereas her works like *Stree Vilap* (1881), *Seemantani Upadesh* (1882), travel memoirs like *London Yatra* (1888) and *London Jubilee* (1889), novels like *Hukmadevi* (1892), treatise like Social Injustice on Women (1892) are of great importance not only historically but from feminist point of view—- these are the early texts in hindi. For women education, She started a magazines called *'Bharat Bhagini'* (1889-1906) in Hindi and Urdu and established institution like *Nari Shilpalaya* (women Polytechnic:1902) for making women economically independent by imparting technical skills and laid the foundation of *Sundari Ashram* to provide shelters for helpless old

---

265 Quoted in V.D.Mahajan, Modern Indian Political Thought. S.Chand & Company, New Delhi, 1987, P.176

widows in Lahore. In nineteenth-century India when there were few examples of women-led societies, such as Pandita Ramabai (1958–1922)'s *Arya Mahila Samaj* (1882) in Pune or Swarna Kumari Devi (1855–1932)'s *Sakhi Samiti* (1886) in Calcutta, In 1885, Hardevi, along with Hemant Kumari Devi (1868-1953), formed the *Vanita Buddhi Vikasini Sabha* in Lahore.

Hemant Kumari Devi (1868-1953), known as the first woman journalist in Hindi in the latter half of the nineteenth century, worked tirelessly to raise women's issues and for women's education. She was the daughter of the famous educationist, Hindi lover and Brahmo Samaj leader Babu Navin Chandra Rai (1837-1890). Hemant Kumari Devi spent most of her life working for women empowerment while living in Lahore, Agra, Ratlam, Shillong, Sylhet, Patiala and Dehradun. She also wrote some booklets for women education, such as *Mata Aur Kanya, Nari Pushpavalli, Naveen Shilp-Mala, Hindi-Bangla Pratham Shiksha* etc. She also wrote a novel named *Adarsh Mata* (1912). In 1888, she started publishing a magazine named *Sughrihini* in Hindi from Ratlam. In the first issue of the magazine, the introduction and objective have been described in a dramatic way: "O dear sisters! Open the door and see who has come to you! Do you people recognize her? She too is a sister of yours. Her name is 'Sugrihini'. Seeing your sorrows, seeing you bound in ignorance and servitude, this sister of yours has come to your door." Further a shloka is quoted: *"Vidyaa saadhvitayaa naari bhushya'alankrita yado,/tad vibhushitam manye natu hemen bhushitam."* That is, when a woman is adorned with the ornaments of knowledge and chastity, then I consider her to be *accomplished.* She is not *accomplished* just by being adorned with gold."[266] But

266 Mangla Anuja, Patrakarita ke yug nirmata Hemantkumari Devi Chaudhari, Prabhat Prakashan, Delhi, 2010, pp.78-79

newspapers and magazines can be successful only where a certain level of literacy has been established whereas the Hindi speaking region was very backward in terms of education, especially in the matter of women education and this used to pain Hemant Kumari Devi a lot. She writes, "Girls of Bengal and Madras are getting higher education, but till date no Hindu north-Indian woman has appeared for the university examination. Women of Calcutta, Bombay etc. have passed the higher university examinations and received degrees like men. One of the main reasons for this is that Bengali and Marathi are respected in the universities of the above mentioned states. If Hindi gets the same treatment in Allahabad University, then there will be love and efforts for women also to pass the entrance examination."[267] In the Hindi belt (United Provinces), till the first decade of the twentieth century, only 1.3 percent of the girls of school-going age were getting any kind of education—this situation was very pathetic even in comparison to other provinces of India[268] and on top of that, instead of new schools opening, they were closing down. When two hundred girls' schools were closed in the North-Western Province, Bhartendu Harishchandra (1850-1885) reminded the government of its duty to remove people's indifference towards women's education before the Hunter Education Commission.[269] If we look at Hindi literature

267 Ibid, quoted on p. 81

268 Bombay;7.2, Madras;6.8, Bengal:4.3, Punjab;3.1% of girls of school age are receiving education' Minna G.Cowan, The Education of the Women of India, Fleming H. Revell Company, New York Chicago Toronto, 1912, p.252

269 "It is true the natives of this country do not wish to educate their females at public schools, but it is the duty of our government to remove the ignorance from their mind." Report by the Provincial Committee representing the North Western Provinces & Oudh in the Education Commission, Government Printing Calcutta, 1884, p.208

of the second half of the nineteenth century, then the rise of women's writing of that time should also be seen in this context. The sensibility created by women writers through their novels, stories and poems, appears to be sensitize the contemporary women issues. Whether it is Mallika Devi's *Kumudini* (1878-82) or *Chandra Prabha aur Poorna Prakash* (1888) or Shrimati Hardevi's *Hukmadevi* (1892) or the poems of Rajrani Devi (1869-1928), questions related to women (mismatched marriages, polygamy, widow remarriage, women's education) have been raised in all of them. What is pertinent to say is that even in the second half of the nineteenth century, issues related to women were blazing in the Hindi region.[270]

Historian Partha Chatterjee has shown in the context of Bengal that with the development of nationalism, issues related to women gradually started fading away, because nationalism considered the women question as an internal problem of Hindu society and was in favour of solving it, as if it was a domestic problem, which had to be solved in the home by the people of the home itself, so now there was no need for any interference from outside (colonial law and order). After considering the colonial West as materially superior, declaring itself spiritually sovereign and free from slavery was such a strategy of Indian nationalism in which the center of spirituality could be considered home and the center of home was women, who could move forward only by considering them autonomous. This is the reason that in the latter half of the nineteenth century, the question of women's liberation seems to have disappeared

270 It is not correct as Neeta Kumar said that women issues were not included in the reformist-nationalist discourse in united province before 1920s. see, Widows, Education and Social Change in Twentieth Century Banaras, Economic and Political Weekly, April, 27, 1991

from the public agenda of the nationalist movement.[271] It is not known how appropriate this was for Bengal, but it was certainly not true for the Hindi region. In this context, sociologist Maitrayee Chaudhary is noteworthy, when she says, "This needs reiteration, for the widespread circulation of Partha Chatterjee's nationalist resolution of the women's question in global academia appears to have truly wiped out the story of political action and resistance of Indian woman (Chatterjee, 1990). This is perhaps a good instance of the limits of textual analysis, where the lure of the conceptual binary of the 'inner' and 'outer', the 'spiritual' and 'material', clearly took precedence over the actual struggles of feminist movements."[272] There is no doubt that the nineteenth century was a period when issues related to women became matters of utmost importance and Radha Kumar is right in saying that "The nineteenth century was a period in which the rights and wrongs of women became major issues. If early attempts at reforming the condition under which Indian Women lived were largely conducted by men, by the late nineteenth century their wives, sisters, daughters, protégés and others affected by campaigns, such as that for women's education had themselves joined in movements. By the early twentieth century women's own autonomous organizations began to be formed and within a couple of decades by the thirties and forties, a special category of 'women's activism' was constructed."[273]

---

271 Partha Chatterjee, *The Nationalist Resolution of the Women's Question*, in *Empire & Nation*, Permanent Black, Ranikhet, First Paperback Printing 2012, pp.120-126

272 Maitrayee Chaudhuri, Feminism in India: The Tales and its Telling, Revue Tiers Monde, No. 209, FÉMINISMES DÉCOLONIAUX, GENRE ETDÉVELOPPEMENT (janvier-mars 2012), Publications de la Sorbonne, p.27 Stable URL: https://www.jstor.org/stable/23593740, Accessed: 23-08-2018 08:38 UTC

273 Radha Kumar, The History of Doing, Kali for Women, First Published 1993, P.1

In the Hindi regi on, the work of Mrs. Hardevi and Hemant Kumari Devi was further carried forward in the first few decades of the twentieth century by the women of Nehru family, particularly Indrani (Nand Ran i) Nehru (1851-1890), Kamla Dar Nehru (1882-19??), Lado Rani Nehru (1882-1968), Uma Hukku Nehru (1884-1963), Rame shwari Raina Nehru (1886-1966), Roop Kumari Nehru (190 1-190?). In this context, the role of women of Nehru family i s, to some extent, comparable to the women of Thakur families o f Bengal[274] — especially Gyandanandini Devi (1850-1941), Swa rn Kumari Devi (1855-1932), Sarla Devi (1872-1945), Sus hmasundari. The publication of *Strī Darpan* by Rameshwari Nehru and the formation of *Prayag Mahila Samiti* in 1909 was a remar kable event for the Hindi region. The decision to publish *Strī Darpan* in Hindi, to raise issues related to women's question was und oubtedly a progressive step. Rameshwari Nehru used to edit *Str ī Darpan* and Kamla Dar Nehru was responsible for its manageme nt[275]. Editor Rameshwari Nehru was very clear about the magazine's goal and its aim. She writes, "To give Indian women a human status has been the goal of this magazine from the

---

274 It is unfortunate that the works of all the women of the Nehru family have not been documented in the same way as those of the women of the Thakur family, for example see Chitra Deb, Women of Tagore Household, Penguin India, first published, 2010. The Nehru Memorial Museum Library has material on Rameshwari Nehru, Vijay Lakshmi Pandit, Indira Gandhi but nothing on Uma Nehru, Lado Rani Nehru, and Roopkumari Nehru. According to Elena Borgi, this 'synonymous memory' cannot be a mere coincidence. See, Elena Borghi, 'Forgotten Feminisms: Gender and the Nehru Household in Early-Twentieth-Century India', Gender & History, Vol.29 No.2 August 2017, pp. 255

275 a supplementary magazine 'Kumari Darpan' also started being published From 1916, the editing of which was undertaken by Rameshwari Nehru and Roopkumari Nehru.

very beginning. ... This goal can be achieved in two ways. One is by changing the thoughts of men towards women and the other is by awakening of women themselves. *Darpan* is constantly trying to achieve both these things through its small efforts. In this paper, while the duties of men towards women are shown, the attention of women is also drawn to their immense responsibility."[276]It is true that along with *Stree Darpan*, many other women-centric, women-edited magazines like *Grihalakshmi* (1910) edited by Gopal Devi, *Stree-Dharma-Shikshak* (1909) edited by Yashoda Devi, *Arya Mahila* (1918) edited by Surath Kumari Devi were published, but the commitment and integrity with which *Stree Darpan* kept raising the women's issue, especially during the editorship of Rameshwari Nehru, is inspiring.

In order to raise women's issues loudly, apart from newspapers and magazines, the formation of assemblies and committees had started in the 19th century itself, such as the *Arya Mahila Samaj* (1882) established by Pandita Rama Bai in Pune and the *Sakhi Samiti* (1896) of Swarn Kumari Devi in Bengal, but the Hindi region remained largely untouched by it. From this point of view, the formation of *Prayag Mahila Samiti* was an event awaited and expected for years. In the February 1910 issue of *Strī Darpan*, it is reported in following words: "We write this news with great pleasure that the society which we women of Prayag had been thinking of forming for a long time, was finally established by some sisters together on the 22nd of last month in the name of *Prayag Mahila Samiti*. On the invite of Mrs. Dhanraj Rani Sapru, about 50 women gathered in her place. On the request of Mrs. Kailasrani Vatal and with the consent of all the sisters, Mrs. Nandrani Nehru was made the president. She told all the gathering that the intention of

276 Stree Darpan, July 1915, pp.1-2

Mrs. Dhanraj rani in calling all the women was that we must form such a society where we often get an opportunity to meet each other. Thereafter, the editor of *Stree Darpan* told what the need of forming this Sabha was and said that women's Sabhas have been formed in every big city. Women have organised meetings in Lahore, Delhi, Dehra, Bombay, Poona, Calcutta, everywhere. But no such Sabha has been formed in Prayag till date, this shows that we women of Prayag are lagging behind. Such a Sabha was needed in Prayag for a long time, today is a day of great fortune that we have all gathered to fulfil this deficiency. "The meeting of this committee will be held on the first of every English month at the house of one of the members. In this meeting, one lady will present a paper on a specific topic and the rest of the ladies will express their opinion on it. Its first meeting will be held at the place of Shri Prayagdas's wife, *Shanti Ashram* and Mrs. Kailasrani Vatal will present a paper on 'mother tongue'. We think that this meeting will be very beneficial for the women society and they will be inspired to think about other things apart from household chores and think about their good and bad. It is hoped that the sisters will try to make this meeting a success and the number of its members will increase every day."[277] Along with the development of nationalism in the early decades of the twentieth century, the consciousness of women's issues has also spread at the all-India level. Sarla Devi disturbed by the male leadership of the National Social Conference, founded the *Bharat Stree Mahamandal* in Lahore in 1910, which also had branches in Allahabad and Calcutta. In 1917, Annie Besant, Margaret Cousins and Dorothy Jinrajdas, Malati Patwardhan, Ammu Swaminathan, Shrimati Dadabhai and Shrimat Ambujammal founded the Women's Indian Association in Madras. Radha Kumar has rightly noted that,

277 Stree Darpan, February 1910

"The decade of 1910-1920 was one in which the first attempts at setting up all-India women's organizations were made. The earliest women's organization were, as we have seen, both urban and sectarian in a non-pejorative sense, for they were Arya Samajist or Brahmo. From the late nineteenth to early twentieth century, they were followed by local or local or regional women's organizations, such as Banga Mahila Samaj and Aghorekamini Nari Samiti in Bengal, the Satara Abalonnati Sabha in Maharashtra, the Mahila Seva Samaj in Bangalore, the Bharat Mahila Parishad in Banaras and the Prayag Mahila Samiti in Allahabad."[278] At the all-India level, the National Council of Indian Women (NCWI) was formed in 1925 and the All India Women's Conference (AIWC) was formed in 1927. This was the time of Gandhian constructive experiments in politics and personalities like Sarla Devi Chaudhrani (1872-1946), Sarojini Naidu (1879 -1949), Kamala Devi Chattopadhyay (1903-1990), Aruna Asaf Ali (1909-1996) were trying to solve the complex equation and contradiction of nationalism and feminism at the all-India level in their own ways. For the first time in India, women were seen becoming active in public life in large numbers. After the Swadeshi Movement (1905-1911), the presence of women in public life during the Non-Cooperation Movement (1918-1920), Civil Disobedience (1930-1934) and Quit India Movement (1942) was no less remarkable in the Hindi region. Sudha Chauhan underlines this fact in the biography of her mother Subhadra Kumari Chauhan (1904-1948) in following words, "Due to the work done by my mother among women, the participation of women in the Congress meetings in Jabalpur used to be nearly 25 percent. Even today, except for a few selected meetings of very big leaders, very few women attend the public meetings and most of whom grace the stage. The public meetings of Jabalpur held in 1930-32 or 1941-42

278 Radha Kumar, Ibid, p.54

were exceptional in the sense that a very large number of women used to gather there, which was a new experience for the Hindi speaking areas. ... Behind this awakening of women, the continuous efforts of my mother and the team prepared by her certainly had some hand. Since 1920, she had been speaking in the meetings of women against purdah, against blind customs, in favor of removal of untouchability and in favor of promoting women education."[279]

Generally it is believed that the feminist movements in the third world almost always arise from the same historical ground and historical moment as nationalism.[280] But perhaps it is also true that after going some distance together, the paths of both are forced to separate. An ideological struggle on the women issues had been going on for years between British imperialism and Indian nationalism in which the contradictions between nationalism and feminism were often ignored by saying that, India cannot be independent until its women become independent and women cannot be independent until India becomes independent.[281]. In such a situation, Katherine Mayo's (1867-1940) book *Mother India* (1927) was published which not only gave rise to a fierce nationalist reaction but also provided feminism an opportunity to recognize its position and define itself in front of nationalism. In *Mother India,* the plight of the majority of women has been considered the main reason for the plight of India and for which the

---

279 Sudha Chauhan, Mila Tej se Tej, Hans Prakashan, Allahabad, 1975, pp.167-68

280 Geraldine Here, A Great Way to fly: Nationalism, the State and the varieties of Third World Feminism in M. Jacqui Alexander and Chandra Talpade Mohanty,(eds.) Feminist Genealogies, Colonial Legacies, Democratic Futures, Routledge, London & New York, 1997, p.31

281 Mrinalini Sinha (ed.) Selection from Mother India, Kali for Women Press, New Delhi, 1998, p.1

internal structure of Hindu civilization, especially the sex-oriented organization of Hindu society, was held responsible. As is clear from Manoranjan Jha's study, American journalist Katherine Mayo definitely wrote Mother India with the intention of propaganda keeping in mind the British imperialist interests[282]. But this work had created a strange dilemma for feminism. On one hand, the criticism of this work could have led to the glorification of the so-called proud Indian woman by going into the lap of nationalists, forgetting the real condition of women, while expressing sympathy with the pathetic condition of women depicted would have meant ultimately strengthening the side of the British imperialists. If we look at the reactions of that period, then barring a few exceptions like Cornelia Sorabji (1866 - 1954), most of the supporters of feminism, showing rare maturity, presented a scathing criticism of *Mother India*, but at the same time also laid great emphasis on the need to improve the deplorable condition of Indian women. As a reaction to Mother India, more than fifty books and booklets were published — in Indian languages like Hindi, Urdu, Marathi, Bengali, Tamil, Telugu as well as in European languages[283]. But only a few works were written by women themselves and that too in Indian languages, probably appeared only in Hindi and that too in couple — Chandravati Lakhanpal[284] wrote a reply to Mother India

282 Manoranjan Jha, Katherine Mayo and India, People's Publishing House, New Delhi, 1971

283 Mrinalini Sinha, ibid, p.2

284 Chandravati Lakhanpal (1904-1969) was born in Bijnor in 1904. Her father's name was Pandit Jayanarayan Shukla. Education: M.A. B.T. from Gurukul Kangri University, Dehradun. In 1926, she married Satyavrat Sidhantalankar (1898-1992), a scholar of Vedic literature. Active participation in the Civil Disobedience Movement. Imprisonment for one year. After independence, she became Member of Parliament in the Rajya Sabha from the Uttar Pradesh Congress Party for nearly ten years (from

in December 1927, as soon as Mother India was published and the next year in 1928, an illustrated Hindi translation of Uma Nehru's (1884-1963) book *Mother India* was also published, which included "Introduction written by Uma Nehru with few talks with Miss Mayo regarding Western imperialism and India". This was not only a proof of the expansion of women's consciousness in the Hindi region, but it is also a beautiful example of how feminism can rise above the logic of nationalism and imperialism and be open for self-criticism. Uma Nehru has written in the preface of the illustrated Hindi translation of Mother India: "Seeing the picture of our country that has been presented before the world, not only the Western nationals but even our own people are shocked. Thrills arise. Just as a vulture looks down from the sky but is not attracted by the thousands of huge trees spread on the earth, the lakhs of fragrant flowers painted in divine colours and the numerous interesting, tasty and healthy nuts and fruits—but when its eyes fall on a dead animal or the corpse of a human being, it immediately gathers its wings and descends towards the earth like a falling iron ball and on getting its wish, it eats its stinking flesh and rotten veined buttocks with the same pleasure, taste and interest, similarly, the mother of *Mother India*, taking encouragement from her community, has searched and described the imaginary and real hateful problems of India with a terrifying and strange interest."[285] But the author further presented a rare example of self-criticism and wrote that "If our real condition is depicted in it, then it should be our religious

---

3-4-1952 to 2-4-1956 and from 3-4-1956 to 2-4-1962). Died on March 31st 1969. Her works are : 'Mother India ka Jawaab' (1927), Striyon ki Sthiti (1934), Shikshaa Manovigyaan (1934) and 'Shiksha Shastra' written jointly with her husband Satyavrat Sidhantalankar.

285 Uma Nehru, Miss Mayo ki Mother India (Sachitra Hindi Anuvaad), Hindustan Press, Allahabad, 1928, pp.8-9

duty to read it and get it read by others. If there are exaggerations and lies in this book, then the western world may be deceived by it, but we ourselves cannot be deceived by it. Hating our faults is the first step to remove them. And those who are afraid of seeing their faults, they themselves nourish their disease with their blood like a sick person who does not take medicine."[286] This is what called the discretion of self-criticism in evaluation and recognition of action in words! This becomes clearer when we compare it with other contemporary works written on *Mother India* as C.S. Ranga Iyer's *Father India*[287], K. Natarajan's *Rejoinder*[288], Lala Lajpat Rai's *Unhappy India*[289] or Dhan Gopal Mukherjee's *'A Son of Mother India Answers*[290] or Shantaram Ganpatrao Varti's *Sister India*[291], Charulata Devi's *The Fair Sex of India: A Reply to Mother India*[292]—these works while written in English, keeping in mind the readers of England and America tries to lay great emphasis on the projected image of India, whereas Chandravati Lakhanpal and Uma Nehru's work appears to recognize the evils of society in front of her Hindi readers and demands its proper addressal. Neither straight acceptance nor right away refusal—This is the wisdom of fair scrutiny, and that is visible in all their work.

---

286 Ibid, pp.10-11

287 C.S.Ranga Iyer, Father India, Selvyn & Blount Ltd, London, 1927

288 K.Natrajan, Miss Mayo's Mother India: A Rejoinder, G.A.Natesan & Co.Madras, 1927

289. Lala Lajpat Rai, Unhappy India, Banna Publishing Co., Calcutta, 1928

290. D.G.Mukherji, A Son of Mother India Answers, E.P.Dutton & Company, New York, U.S.A.1928

291. Shantaram Ganpatrau Warty, Sister India, Sister India Office, Bombay, 1928

292. Charulata Devi, The Fair Sex of India: A Reply to "Mother India", Ramakrishna Cottage, Calcutta, 1929

In an interesting hypothetical question-answer session titled *A couple of things with Miss Mayo about Western imperialism and India*, Uma Nehru appears to debate with Miss Mayo in such a way that it becomes an excellent example of criticism along with the excitement of true polemics. The debate begins like this: "Miss Mayo, I have heard that India was once considered one of the civilized countries of the world. Other countries could not compete with it in artistic skill and industrial progress. Whatever things it needed to make its life comfortable, it used to make them on its own. Merchants from other countries used to take the products made here to far off countries in ships that was made in this country. Gold and silver from other countries used to come to this country like the endless flow of a huge river. Miss Mayo, why has this world famous merchant become a beggar like the untouchables and disgusting midwife depicted by you? What happened to all his wealth, his artistic skills, his splendor, his self-respect? Why is famine always here? Why are the unfortunate children of this country so weak and sick? And why have all the terrible epidemics of the world, leaving other countries, made this country their home? Miss Mayo, it may not be correct but in our religious books only one reason has been given for this type of plight of countries. That is:

"When a king starts oppressing his subjects by disrespecting the state system, the era that begins at that point of time is called Kali Yuga. At that time many epidemics start spreading. People start dying prematurely, women become widows, rains do not come on time and the crop yield decreases." Mahabharata, Shanti Parva, Chapter 69, Verse 91-95

"Why Miss Mayo, what you have to say? Is this statement untrue? If it is untrue, then you please tell us the real reason for the downfall of our country?[293]

Further, she discussed the plight of India — its educational, economic and industrial decline in a systematic manner and found that the colonial system was responsible for it. To substantiate her argument, the manner in which she has quoted from the wide range of scholarship in politics, history, social science and journalism- in a manner that proves not only her being widely read but also reveals that the author has accepted theoretical concepts, opinions, postulates, facts etc. only through her own experiences and logic. This kind of preparation and intellectual rigour was rare in Hindi at that point of time, even for a male writer.

This was also a proof of the expansion of women's consciousness in the Hindi region, but it is also a beautiful example of how feminism can rise above the logic of nationalism and imperialism and present itself for self-criticism. Chandravati Lakhanpal writes in the book's preface (two words): "Many of Miss Mayo's statements are lies, not only lies, but dirty and vile, but after turning the pages of this book, can anyone deny that many of her statements are true as well, and it pains my heart to write that they are absolutely true. I want this book to reach every person in India and everyone should know that while Miss Mayo left no stone unturned in lying to defame us, she also left no stone unturned in telling the truth in some places! Reader, turn the pages of the book in the echo of these words and keep emitting sparks from your eyes to burn the filth of your society. This is the real answer of 'Mother India'!"[294] This

---

293 Uma Nehru, ibid

294 Chandravati Lakhanpal, Mother India Ka Jawab, Gurukul Kangri, Dehradun, 1927, p.2

proposed answer of Mother India is not only emotional, but also sensible.

The critical view that scholar like Uma Nehru and Chandravati Lakhanpal has shown towards the western values in colonial India is also worth noting. After the reply to *Mother India*, Chandravati Lakhanpal's next work *Striyon ki Sthiti* (1934), begins with this proclamation, "Like my western sisters, I want freedom, and I want it very strongly, but I do not love western values. We have to learn the spirit of freedom from them, but we have to keep our own ideals. Instead of running after only the east or only the west, I would like the status of women should be conceived by combining what is true, good and beautiful in both."[295] Today, when the feminist discourse in Hindi is going through a period of confusion, these lines can serve as a guideline. It is also necessary today that we try to listen to the heard and not- so- heard voices of our colonial past, its silences, its proclamations, its murmur — lest what we had considered 'irrelevant' in the deafening narrative of Bengal-centric renaissance and moved on, not only could be relevant today but may appear to be significant and insightful. To get acquainted with the cultural history of the Hindi region, it is necessary to know the history of the women's struggle of this region and to know the history of women's struggle, it is necessary to know the works produced during this struggle.

295 Chandravati Lakhanpal, Striyon ki Sthiti, Ganga Pustak Karyalaya, Luchnow, 1934, pp.3-4

12

Tradition of Resistance Poetry in Khari Boli Hindi

The emergence of Khari Boli Hindi is the outcome of its confrontation and resistance to two well established poetry traditions of north India in 19th century—namely, Braj Bhasha and Urdu. The whole Khari Boli Hindi movement (1886-1920)[296] was aimed towards making one single language for the masses and for the literature and therefore the earlier division of separate language for the court, urban elites and bureaucracy (Urdu) and separate language for intercourse amongst rural masses (Khari Boli); different language for poetry (Braj Bhasha) and different language for prose (Khari Boli) was resisted vehemently. Noted Hindi Writer Sachchidanand Vatsyayan rightly pointed out that, "*Hindi from very beginning has been anti-establishment, neither the establishment ever tried to patronize it nor it got any reason to think that there could be in any way any proximity to the establishment. This feeling of resistance has given this language a tremendous confidence —in midst of deep religiosity it made conscious to the importance of common folk. Till the independence the anti-establishment autonomous character of Hindi remained intact...after independence, it appeared for few days as if Hindi will be adopted by the establishment and therefore some kind of hesitation prevailed but it did not last long. To deliberate*

296 See, Shitikanth Mishra, Khari Boli Ka Andolan, Kashi Nagri Pracharini Sabha, Varanasi, 1956, p.350

upon its reason here is not important. What is important here to emphasize is that even preserving its fundamental role as a language of anti-establishment, Hindi could also fulfill its role as a language which preserves tradition."[297] It is true that Khari Boli Hindi had no state patronage or religious backings but masses liked it and it is no surprise that Frederic Pincott (1836-1896) admitted in 1888 that, "*The progress of Khari Boli has, hitherto, not been so marked as that of Urdu, because it has had to rely on its natural strength for any development it has attained. It has lacked the fostering hand of Government patronage, and has been generally neglected even by the natives themselves, as they esteem it the uncourtly idiom of the vulgar. During the last twenty years, however, it has steadily forced itself more and more into attention, as its flexibility, terseness, strength, vigour, and richness have become more clearly recognized by scholars.*"[298] It will be no exaggeration, if we add that these adjectives or attributes to Khari Boli Hindi are clearly the outcome of its anti-establishment endeavours and resistance.

The emergence of Khari Boli Hindi coincides with the rise of nationalism in India and it soon became one of the most powerful vehicle to resist the colonial hegemony. No wonder N. Gerald Barrier, in his classic study on banned Indian literature under British rule noted, "Indian nationalism fostered an outpouring of patriotic poetry and songs, probably the largest single category of

297 Sachchidanand Vatsyayan, Adyatan, Saraswati Vihar, Delhi, Second Edition 1978, pp.158-159

298 Frederic Pincott, preface of Ayodhya Prasad Khatri's edited first anthology of Khari Boli Hindi (Khari Boli ka Padya: 1887) in Ramniranjan Parimalendu(ed.) Khadi Boli ka Padya, Sahitya Akademi, First edition, 2008, p.52

printed matter confiscated by the British."[299]He further elaborated that Out of three thousand nine hundred and eight (3908) banned Indian literary works listed in National Archives of India, The British Museum and the India office Library, the number of Hindi works is one thousand seven hundred and eleven (1711).[300] This data proves the point about language's emerging power to resist and withstand colonial onslaught and give voice to the sentiments of voiceless. One of the banned patriotic songs proclaims: *Tyrants have arrogance for their weapons/whereas we have only vande mataram. /Killer, daren't kill us, by our blood/vande mataram will be testimony on your weapons. / Even sentries are restless whereas every rattle/ from the prison utters vande mataram.*[301] The phrase *Vande Mataram (Hail Motherland),* coined by Bankim Chandra Chattopadhyay (1838-1894) *in 1870s* though it later became controversial[302] soon became a catchword for anti-colonial resistance in its glorious phase. Historian R.C.Majumdar has pointed out that, "During the long and arduous struggle for freedom from 1905 to 1947 'Bande Mataram' was the rallying cry of the patriotic sons of India, and thousands of them succumbed to the lathi blow of the British

---

299 N. Gerald Barrier, BANNED Controversial Literature and Political Control in British India 1907-1947, Manohar Delhi, p.270

300 Ibid, p.167

301 जालिमों को है उधर बंदूक अपनी पर गरूर,/है इधर हम बेकसों का तीर वंदे मातरम् ।/कत्ल कर हमको न कातिल तू, हमारे खून से,/तेग पर हो जाएगा तहरीर वंदे मातरम् ।संतरी भी मुज़्तरिब है जबकि हर झंकार से,/बोलती है जेल में जंजीर वंदे मातरम् । विश्वनाथ शर्मा, देखें, रामजन्म शर्मा (सम्पा.), जब्तशुदा गीत:आज़ादी और एकता के तराने, प्रकाशन विभाग, दिल्ली, 2021, पृष्ठ 6

302 See, Tanika Sarkar, Birth of a Goddess: 'Vande Mataram', "Anandamath", and Hindu Nationhood, Economic and Political Weekly, Sep. 16-22, 2006, Vol. 41, No. 37 (Sep. 16-22, 2006), pp. 3959-3969 and A. G. Noorani, Vande Mataram: A Historical Lesson, Economic and Political Weekly, Jun. 9, 1973, Vol. 8, No. 23 (Jun. 9, 1973), pp.1039+1041-1043

police or mounted the scaffold with 'Bande Mataram' on their lips."[303] During anti-colonial struggle the deification of motherland later incorporated not only the deification of national heroes like Mahatma Gandhi, Jawaharlal Nehru, Subhash Chandra Bose, Bhagat Singh etc. but their heroic agendas for national liberation too acquired deified status. No wonder, the literature of this period is full of poems on these national heroes and their anti-colonial programmes like Satyagraha, Swadeshi, non-violence, spinning wheel, non-cooperation, Azad Hind Fauj and Dilli Chalo etc.[304] One poem of this phase, published in 1922 begins with: *The uproar of Satyagraha is everywhere/Everyone has decided to enroll its volunteer/ everyone has decided to defy rules what honored earlier/by calling us insurgent, strife is born/welcome is rebellion as we don't need favors.*[305] *Yet* in an another poem based on Subhash Chandra Bose's call *Dilli Chalo* reiterates it in such words: *Let us march to Delhi as this is the call of our country/ Let us march to Delhi as this is the call of our Nation/ Let us march to Delhi as this is the call of our soul/suffering became music for the inspiration/grief too turned reign for sentiments/penance became crown for soldiers/Bravery calls us not to be in abeyance.*[306]The

---

303 Quoted in A. G. Noorani, ibid, p.1039

304 देखें, भवानीप्रसाद गुप्त(सम्पादक), स्वतंत्रता की पुकार, साहित्योदय कार्यालय, इलाहाबाद, 1923 ; राजेश कुमार परती (सम्पादक), देशभक्ति के गीत(ब्रिटिश राज द्वारा प्रतिबंधित साहित्य से), राष्ट्रीय अभिलेखागार, नई दिल्ली, 1985 ;मीना अग्रवाल (सम्पादक), चुने हुए राष्ट्रीय गीत, विद्या विहार, नई दिल्ली, 1992

305 है धूम मची सत्याग्रह की /सेवक दल में नाम लिखैये, यही राय है सब की /कानूनों की करें अवज्ञा, इज्जत करते थे जिनकी /सेवक संघ बतायो बागी, जड़ बोई है विग्रह की/यह बागीपन रहै मुबारक हमें न चाह अनुग्रह की/है धूम मची सत्याग्रह की। देखें, शिवशंकर मिश्र, सिद्ध गोपाल शुक्ल, गजब की होली या राष्ट्रीय फाग, भारती भण्डार, कानपुर, प्रथम संस्करण 1922, पृष्ठ 6

306 देश की पुकार यही दिल्ली चलें हम/राष्ट्र की पुकार, यही दिल्ली चलें हम,/प्राण की पुकार यही दिल्ली चलें हम/ वन्दना के गाने में नव-गान छिपा है, /बंदियों के प्राण में बलिदान छिपा है,/साधकों के ध्यान में वरदान छिपा है,/आज युग कराहता कि दुष्ट दलें हम। Sushil Kumar Tiwari(compilation), Poems and Songs on Azad Hind Fauj &Subhash Chandra Bose, IGNOU, New Delhi, 2023, p.112

wish to merge *Country, Nation* with the soul of oneself is the most characteristic feature of these patriotic songs and most of such Poems written during this period were banned for its moving political connotations and literary historians could hardly take note of it[307], but there were also some other kind of poems that was resistant to traditional literary —like accepted Protagonist or conventional forms— and social values like feudalism and capitalism prevalent at that point of time. This is the time when Progressive Writer's Association emerged.

Gaya Prasad Shukla 'Sanehi' (1883-1972) wrote a poem titled 'Samyavad' (communism) in 1921, where it was demanded that, *everyone should get equal rights on material possessions/Be it farming or crafts or trade or education.*[308] In a highly hierarchical, semi feudal and semi capitalist society, this was a demand that was unheard of, even communist party of India and Progressive Writers' Conference, was yet to be formed at that point of time. There was something in the air that even romantic poet like Sumitranandan Pant started wishing, *Fall fast the outworn leaves of the world*[309] *and* Suryakant Tripathi *Nirala* in a poem was over joyous by saying

307 Prof. Manager Pandey rightly pointed out that writer of these works were doubly punished as it was not only banned by the British in colonial times but it was completely ignored in post-colonial India too. In the literary history of Hindi, written by right from the great Ramchandra Shukla (Hindi Sāhitya ka Itihas:1929) to Ramswaroop Chaturvedi(Hindi Sāhitya aur Samvedana ka Vikas:1986), not a single banned work was ever discussed. See, https://www.apnimaati.com/2022/11/blog-post_36.html (accessed on 13.7.2023)

308 सांसारिक सम्पत्ति पर सबका सम अधिकार हो,/वह खेती या शिल्प हो विद्या या व्यापार हो ॥ http://kavitakosh.org/kk/ साम्यवाद /गयाप्रसाद शुक्ल स्नेही ((accessed on 13.7.2023)

309 द्रुत झरो जगत के जीर्ण पत्र, युगांत, इंद्र प्रिंटिंग वर्क्स, अल्मोढा, 19 34, पृष्ठ 1

that *mansions of affluent will be turned into school for peasants and the downtrodden— Dhobi, pasi, chamar, teli— will open the lock of darkness* .[310] Similarly poets like Balkrishna Sharma *Navin*, Shivmangal Singh *Suman*, Ramdhari Singh *Dinkar*, Harivansh Rai *Bachchan*, Nagarjun, Kedarnath Agarwal, Trilochan opposed the current decadent social value system vehemently in their work and emphasized the need for socialist values of equality and social justice. No wonder, Munshi Premchand delivering presidential Address at the first All India Progressive Writers' Conference, held at Lucknow on 10th April 1936, proclaimed, *The literature of our immediate past had nothing to do with actuality; our writers were living in a world of dreams and were writing things like Fasanai Ajaib or Chandra Kanta; tales told only for entertainment, or to satisfy our sense of wonder. Life and literature were considered to be two different things which bore no relation to each other. Literature reflects the age. In the past days of decadence the main function of literature was to entertain the parasitic class. In this literature the dominant notes were either sex or mysticism, pessimism or fatalism. It was devoid of vigour, originality, and even the power of observation. But our literary taste is undergoing a rapid transformation. It is coming more and more to grips with the realities of life; it interests itself with society or man as a social unit. It is not satisfied now with the singing of frustrated love; or with writing to satisfy only our sense of wonder; it concerns itself with the problems of our life; and such themes as have a social value. The literature which does not arouse in us a critical spirit, or satisfy our spiritual and intellectual needs, which is not 'force-giving' and dynamic, which does not awaken our sense of beauty, which does not*

---

310 आओ, आओ।/आज अमीरों की हवेली /किसानों की होगी पाठशाला, /धोबी, पासी, चमार, तेली /खोलेंगे अँधेरे का ताला, /एक पाठ पढ़ेंगे, टाट बिछाओ। रामविलास शर्मा,(सम्पादक), राग-विराग, लोकभारती प्रकाशन, इलाहाबाद, पृष्ठ 158

make us face the grim realities of life in a spirit of determination, has no use for us today. It cannot even be termed as literature.[311]This new progressive poetics induced a kind of literature that was egalitarian in their outlook and resistant to all kind of orthodoxy albeit all poets were not Marxist or communist, though poets like Shamsher Bahadur Singh heralded that *left, Left, Left is the direction/Epoch is Communist/Left is Partisan/Epoch: communist.*[312]It is true that these kind of wishful thinking that was illusionary in nature led to a kind of poetry where revolution was just around the corner but it was also, in some way an effort to realize the objectives and dream of PWA as formulated earlier in such words, *It is the object of our association to rescue literature and other arts from the priestly, academic and decadent classes in whose hands they have degenerated so long; to bring the arts into the closest touch with the people; and to make them the vital organs which will register the actualities of life, as well as lead us to the future.*[313]Historically speaking, this was the objective—poetics of Realism— which was followed quite ardently by the poetry of resistance at that point of time.

India got freedom with one of the bloodiest and largest mass migrations of people in history. Poetry could do nothing except to memorialize this failed dream for a non-violent and peaceful postcolonial subcontinent. The day that was meant for mass

311 https://indianhistorycollective.com/munshi-premchand-nature andpurposeofliterature-progressivewritersassociation-faiz-manto-mulkrajanand/(accessed on 13.7.2023)

312 "वाम, वाम, वाम दिशा/समय साम्यवादी ।/वाम-पक्षवादी है.../समय : साम्यवादी।"नामवर सिंह(सम्पादक), शमशेर: प्रतिनिधि कविताएँ, राजकमल प्रकाशन, दिल्ली, पहला संस्करण 1990 पृष्ठ 47 -48

313 Quoted in Raza Mir, Ali Husain Mir, Anthems of Resistance, Indiaink, Roli Books, New Delhi, 2006, p.5

celebration turned out to be a place for condolences, Faiz captured the essence in such words: *This stained light/this day-break, battered by the night/this dawn that we all waited so long /this is not the one./ This is not the one for which we were so sure to see/ believing that Somewhere must be the stars' last halting place/ Somewhere the coast of night's slow tide,/Somewhere a dock for the ship of heart break.*[314] On the very day of independence, Hindi poet Ageya tried to reason out this tragedy in the following lines of the poem, 'Crops are ready': *With laughter in the sewers of enmity/We watered the sand of politics/ Today there are rivers of blood flowing in it/Only yesterday in which we spat by calling it dust/Today the cultivation of hatred has ripened in them/There are next winters to harvest.*[315] In fact the reactions regarding independence in poetry were very wide and diverse in nature. Some poems are celebratory in nature like : *Beloved country of India / your fame spread everywhere / your power is felt all over / By swaying on sky-water-horizon/ your ascendance is glorious / O the grandeur of the sages /My beloved India.*[316] And some poems are expression of quite different sensibilities like: *This independence*

---

314 *यह दाग़ दाग़ उजाला, यह शब-गुज़ीदा -सहर/वह इंतज़ार था जिसका, यह वह सहर तो नहीं। /यह वह सहर तो नहीं जिसकी आरज़ू लेकर/चले थे यार के मिल जाएगी कहीं न कहीं। /फ़लक के दश्त में तारों की आखिरी मंज़िल/कहीं तो होगा शब-ए सुस्त- मौज का साहिल। /कहीं तो जाके रुकेगा सफ़ीना-ए-ग़म-ए-दिल,/जवां लहू की पुर-असरार शाह-राहों से।* Poems by Faiz, Victor Kiernan(Tr.), Vanguard Books, London, 1971, p.123

315 वैर की परनालियों में हँस-हँस के/हमने सींची जो राजनीति की रेती/उसमें आज बह रही खूँ की नदियाँ हैं/कल ही जिसमें ख़ाक-मिट्टी कह के हमने थूका था/घृणा की आज उसमें पक गई खेती/फ़सल कटने को अगली सर्दियाँ हैं पक गई फसल, शरणार्थी, मेरठ, 15 अक्टूबर, 1947 https://www.hindikavita.com/HindiSharanarthiAgyeya.php(accessed on 14.7.2023)

316 प्यारे भारत देश/गगन-गगन तेरा यश फहरा/पवन-पवन तेरा बल गहरा/क्षिति-जल-नभ पर डाल हिंडोले/ चरण-चरण संचरण सुनहरा/ओ ऋषियों के त्वेष/प्यारे भारत देश।।http://kavitakosh.org/kk/प्यारे भारत देश/माखनलाल चतुर्वेदी

is misleading /People of the country are starving.[317]It is also very puzzling to note that very few work of Khari Boli Hindi on partition and independence has been written whereas Khari Boli Urdu has very rich collections and repertoire. Sachchidanand Vatsyayan Ageya is the only major Hindi writer who composed eleven poems under the title *Sharnarthi* (Refugee) during the tumultuous times of 1947 itself. These poems are written with rare sensitivity and unsentimental rationality in response to or perhaps to resist such a situation where such lines were composed— *Run, run, wherever you can/There is no one of your own, Here speed is the only bet / you will die if you rest!*[318] The horror of communal violence is depicted here with abhorrence and simple empathy, quite unlike what American black poet Amiri Baraka (1934–2014) argued in Black Art: *Poems are bullshit unless they are teeth... we want "poems that kill."/Assassin poems, Poems that shoot/guns. Poems that wrestle cops into alleys/and take their weapons leaving them dead/with tongues pulled out and sent to Ireland.*[319]Though Ageya has never been a Gandhian or believer of non-violence, this line of argument would have certainly amused or baffled him!

Post-colonial democratic India experienced a kind of dictatorship during emergency (June 1975 to March 1977).Thousands and thousands people were arrested, sterilized and suppressed, press

317 ये आजादी झूठी है/देश की जनता भूखी है देखें, फणीश्वर नाथ रेणु, मैला आँचल, राजकमल प्रकाशन, दिल्ली 1954, पृष्ठ 134

318 भागो, भागो, चाहे जिस ओर भागो/अपना नहीं है कोई, गति ही सहारा यहाँ-/रुकेंगे तो मरेंगे! https://www.hindikavita.com/HindiSharanarthiAgyeya.php (accessed on 14.7.2023)

319 Selected Poetry of Amiri Baraka/Le Roi Jones, William Morrow & Co, New York, 1979

and media was banned and all opposition was crushed with iron hands. Prime Minister Mrs. Indira Gandhi became synonymous to tyranny. But as it is said bad times are good for poetry, hundreds and hundreds poem were written in every Indian languages to resist this undemocratic regime. Collecting these poems for an anthology, editor John Oliver Perry writes," ...from 1975 to 1977 a considerable amount of protest against Emergency conditions was expressed despite, and often because of, the official censorship and the evident pressures for self-censorship that came from thousands being jailed without charges, trial or appeal. Underground poetry formed part of this protest..."[320] No wonder some underground poetry was also written and published anonymously.one such poem in Hindi goes like this: He: *If you tell lies, the people will peck. /So beware of the black jay now.* She: *well, I'll go to Italy then. /And you'll look for me in vain.* He :*If you go to Italy/I'll bring a warrant for you.*/She: *If you bring a warrant /I'll hide in my villa hotel./* He: *If you hide in the hotel/I'll bring the bulldozers there.*/She: *If you bring the bulldozers / I'll hide in the Maruti.*/He: *If you hide in a Maruti/I'll find you very easily.*/She:*Well, I won't go to Italy then;/I'll join in the Jānata.*[321] These are the poems where pun, rhythm and sarcasm are the main tools for the communication and if you are unaware of the connotation of *black Jaggu, Italy, bulldozers, Maruti* etc.it won't work. Similarly some anonymous poems were composed in Hindi as if it is a folk song, like: *Come on folks listen a story that is*

---

320 John Oliver Perry(ed.), Voices of Emergency, Popular Prakashan, Bombay,, First published, 1983, p.xv

321 झूठ बोले जनता काटे /काले जग्गू से डरियो/मैं इटली चली जाउंगी /तुम देखते रहियो /तू इटली चली जायेगी /मैं वारंट ले के आउंगा/तू वारंट लेकर आयेगा .मैं होटल में घुस जाउंगी /तू होटल में घुस जाएगी मैं बुलडोजर ले के आउंगा /तू बुलडोजर ले के आएगा मैं मारुति में छिप जाउंगी /मैं इटली नहीं जाउंगी/मैं जनता में मिल जाउंगी। Ibid, pp.38-39

not very old. /In a country there was a queen /very clever, very cunning/ two sweet prince she had, spoiled by her fondness./one prince and one queen both started arbitrariness./everyone was shut and whoever spoke sent to prison/ bullets, censor, MISA, canes/ everyone was grinded in these millstones.[322]During election after emergency these poems were turned into street songs that also had tremendous power to entertain and mobilise.But apart from these poems, in response to Emergency, there were usual, literary kind of poetry also composed by contemporary Hindi poets like Bhavani Prasad Mishra, Raghuvir Sahai, Sarveshwar Dayal Saxena, Renu, Dharmaveer Bharti, Kunwar Narain, Shriram Verma, Vinod Bhardwaj, Leeladhar Jagudi, Rajesh Joshi etc. Much of the poems in the collection *Hanso, Hanso, Jaldi Hanso* is in response to the time of emergency, Title poem goes like this: *Laugh as you are being watched. /Laugh but not at yourself as the bitterness will come out /and you'll be killed. /Laugh without looking too happy/or they'll suspect that you don't own the shame. /and you'll be killed.*[323] Similarly Sarveshwar too has captured not only the vicious and oppressive atmosphere of the surrounding but its terrorizing effect too: *All night/a red cycle/stood against the barbed fence/forlorn and alone/shrill whistle of the police blew/heavy boots thudded the ground. /in the morning/a child appeared/and played/with the dew-wet cycle bell./Then/with screaming siren/a huge black van/roared to a stop—The child/forgot his bell/watching in fascination/the winking blue*

322 आओ लोगो सुनो कहानी /बात नहीं है बहुत पुरानी /किसी देश में एक थी रानी /बहुत चतुर और बहुत सयानी/उसके थे दो राजदुलारे बिगड़ गए थे लाड़ के मारे/एक शहजादा एक महारानी /दोनों करते इतने मनमानी/सब के मुख पर जकड़ा ताला/जो भी बोला जेल में डाला /लाठी, गोली, सेंसर, मीसा/इस चक्की में सब को पीसा। quoted in Raj Thapar, The Election, Seminar Annual No. 221, Delhi, Jan 1978, p 40

323 हँसो तुम पर निगाह रखी जा रही है/हँसो अपने पर न हँसना क्योंकि उसकी कड़वाहट पकड़ ली जाएगी/और तुम मारे जाओगे/ऐसे हँसो कि बहुत खुश न मालूम हो/वरना शक होगा कि यह शख़्स शर्म में शामिल नहीं/और मारे जाओगे। हँसो, हँसो, जल्दी हँसो, नेशनल पेपरबैक्स, दिल्ली, द्वितीय संस्करण 1987, पृष्ठ 25

light on its roof.../The black van took away the child. /For the first time/I watched the shadow of the window-bars/on the floor/and was filled with terror.[324]some resistance poetry were written in direct hard hitting manner, without any cover of simile, metaphor, allegory or under any garb of folktales; if you consider Nagarjun's very popular poem 'Indu Ji, What happened to you?' that addresses straight to Mrs. Gandhi with such blunt probing questions: *Indu ji, Indu Ji, What happened to you? / Intoxicated by power did you forget your father? You became habitual testing student's blood/you love buttering by black means/ If someone objected, you felt offended/you cnatter in vehemence /The crapulence of power melted in your blood/ You have considered the sin of murder lighter than a flower / Indu Ji, What happened to you? Capacitated your son, shattered your father!*[325] Basically these are no questions but comments which give confidence and courage to speak, what ought to be spoken without any hesitation and as poet has articulated it by saying: *People are asking to me what to reply/I'm people' poet will speak straight why to stammer.*[326]

Another stream of resistance poetry in Khari Boli Hindi was written against the current malpractices of democracy in contemporary India that was not against democracy *per say* as it can be testified by many references in Dhumil's poetry, one such lines are this: *Democracy in our country is such performance/whose life depends solely on juggler's parlance.*[327] With the rise of far right in

---

324 John Oliver Perry(ed.), ibid, pp.176-177

325 इन्दु जी, इन्दु जी, क्या हुआ आपको? सत्ता की मस्ती में/भूल गई बाप को? छात्रों के लहू का चस्का लगा आपको/काले चिकने माल का मस्का लगा आपको/किसी ने टोका तो ठस्का लगा आपको/अन्ट-शन्ट बक रही जनून में/शासन का नशा घुला ख़ून में/फूल से भी हल्का/समझ लिया आपने हत्या के पाप को/इन्दु जी, क्या हुआ आपको/बेटे को तार दिया, बोर दिया बाप को/ नागार्जुन, खिचडी विप्लव देखा हमने, संभावना प्रकाशन, हापुड़, प्रथम संस्करण, 1980, पृष्ठ 9 -10

326 जनता मुझसे पूछ रही है क्या बतलाऊं /जन कवि हूं मैं साफ कहूंगा क्यों हकलाऊं /शोभाकांत(सम्पादक), नागार्जुन रचनावली, भाग 1, राजकमल प्रकाशन, दिल्ली, प्रथम संस्करण, 2003, पृष्ठ 400

327 अपने यहां लोकतंत्र एक ऐसा तमाशा है/ जिसकी जान/ मदारी की भाषा है। धूमिल, पटकथा, संसद से सड़क तक, राजकमल प्रकाशन, दिल्ली, चौथी आवृत्ति, 2001, पृष्ठ 105

politics a lot of resistance poetry in Hindi is being written against Hindutva forces. These poems challenge the singular interpretation of Hindu religion as such and emphasize the inherent diversity and acquired argumentative nature of Indian civilization. Some of these poems tried to counter the growing intolerance in our society, Rajesh Joshi's poem is one such example : *Will be killed / those who will not join this madness will be killed / will be put in the dock/ Those who will speak in opposition / who will speak the truth will be killed/ will not be tolerated if someone's shirt is whiter than his/Those who don't have stains on their shirts will be killed/Will be pushed out of the art's world, who is not bard /Those who do not sing praises will be killed/ with religion's flag in hand, those who will not join the procession/They will be shot, they will be declared infidels/The Biggest crime right now is /to be unarmed and innocent/who would not be criminal /Will be killed.*[328] This is the darkest and hopeless world of our time and it is expressed in such poetry, hoping that it could lead to comprehend the reality fully so we may think to change it for the better.

---

328 मारे जायेंगे/जो इस पागलपन में शामिल नहीं होंगे, मारे जायेंगे/कठघरे में खड़े कर दिए जाएंगे/जो विरोध में बोलेंगे/जो सच-सच बोलेंगे, मारे जाएंगे/ बर्दाश्त नहीं किया जाएगा कि किसी की क़मीज़ हो/'उनकी' क़मीज़ से ज़्यादा सफ़ेद / क़मीज़ पर जिनके दाग़ नहीं होंगे, मारे जाएँगे/धकेल दिए जाएँगे कला की दुनिया से बाहर, जो चारण नहीं जो गुन नहीं गाएँगे, मारे जाएँगे/धर्म की ध्वजा उठाए जो नहीं जाएँगे जुलूस में/गोलियाँ भून डालेंगी उन्हें, काफ़िर क़रार दिए जाएँगे / सबसे बड़ा अपराध है इस समय/निहत्थे और निरपराध होना/जो अपराधी नहीं होंगे/मारे जाएँगे। राजेश जोशी, प्रतिनिधि कविताएँ, राजकमल प्रकाशन, दिल्ली, संस्करण 2015, पृष्ठ 79

13

Realism and Modernism: Stories of Lu Xun and Muktibodh

It is generally believed that when European modernism was challenging 'realism' in the early and mid-twentieth century, the non-realistic forms of Asian traditional art were emerging as a major source of inspiration for them[329] and it is also true that at about the same time the same realism was being accepted whole-heartedly in Asia and marvelled it as *The fo*rm for its perceived suitability in depicting colonial, semi-colonial or post-colonial reality; the realist forms of European art were considered supreme; but there were some exceptions to it too —- who tried to swim against the so-called mainstream — the sharp realization of the limitations of realism probably inspired them to find new ways and reinvent their age-long non-realist traditional forms[330]. According to them, art does not perceive reality like photography but by revealing what remains invisible in the perceptible form of reality[331]. There can

329 The examples of Bertolt Brecht, Antonin Artaud, and Jerzi Grotovasky et.al are easily cited here.

330 In everyday usage, *reality* refers to the universe that exists independent of our thoughts. Dreams or delusions, which we experience when we are asleep or are otherwise not in full possession of our senses, are examples of the *non-real*. Reality. International Encyclopedia of the Social Sciences .2008. <http: //www .encyclopedia. com

331 Ronald Taylor(edited and translated), Aesthetics and politics, Verso, London, 1980, p.162

be many ways and methods of this *revelation* and in this context the case of Lu Xun's (1881-1936) world famous stories *Diary of a Madman* and *The True Story of IQ* and Muktibodh's (1917-1964) *Claude Etherley and The Disciple of Brahmarakchasa* is a point to be discussed.

Lu Xun's *A Madman's Diary*:

***"Here madness and non-madness, reason and non-reason are inextricably involved: inseparable at the moment when they do not yet exist, and existing for each other, in relation to each other, in the exchange which separates them."* Michel Foucault**[332]

Lu Xun's *A Madman's Diary* (Kuangren riji: 1918) is presented with a small preface by its narrator in the story. The preface is written in classical Chinese (Wenyan) for obvious reason of contextualizing the text in a certain way, whereas *diary* is produced in modern vernacular Chinese (Baihua). When this diary was provided to the preface-writer, he immediately diagnosed the *disease* of the diary-writer and thought useful case for further medical research. If we consider biographical details of the author Lu Xun (1881-1936), we can safely assume that narrator of the diary is author himself. He discloses in the preface, "*I took the diary away, read it through, and found that he had suffered from a form of persecution complex. The writing was most confused and incoherent, and he had made many wild statements; moreover he had omitted to give any dates, so that only by the colour of the ink and the differences in the writing could one tell*

332 Foucault, Michel, Madness and civilization, Vintage Books Edition, New York, 1988, p.10

that it was not written at one time. Certain sections, however, were not altogether disconnected, and I have copied out a part to serve as a subject for medical research."[333]

So this is clear that diary that is being presented to the reading public by the narrator is not complete or value-free text for the reader to form opinion of his/her own but an edited version with highly subjective, differentiated evaluation attached with it.[334] It seems like presenting a case history for psychoanalysis as Sigmund Freud (1856-1939) has presented the case of a German judge Dr. Daniel Paul Schreber (1842 – 1911).[335] Unlike his other famous case histories like *Dora, Little Hans, Rat Man or Wolf Man*, Dr. Schreber had never been a patient of Sigmund Freud but he has analyzed his case on the basis of his published autobiographical work *Memoirs of My Nervous Illness* (original German title *Denkwürdigkeiten eines Nervenkranken*).After presenting Dr.Schreber's case, Freud

333 *Selected Stories of Lu Xun*, Translated by Yang Hsein-hi and Gladys Yang, Oriole Editions, New York, 1972, p.26

334 "*one could follow the madman's lead and treat the diary as a depiction of an infectious disease that literally transforms its victims into cannibals and that is transmitted through the act of consumption; or one might instead follow the narrator's lead and approach the work as a symptom of a delusional mental illness (which the narrator calls "paranoiac schizophrenia" that causes the madman to believe he is surrounded by cannibals. Alternatively, one could follow the scholarly consensus and read the story as an allegorical critique of China's "cannibalistic" illness, or what C. T. Hsia has famously called the nation's "spiritual disease".* Of Canons and Cannibalism: A Psycho-immunological Reading of "Diary of a Madman", Carlos Rojas, Modern Chinese Literature and Culture, Vol. 23, No. 1, Special Issue on Discourses of Disease (Spring, 2011), p. 47

335 *"Lu Xun was the first Chinese writer to know about Freud's theory."* Ning Wang, Freudianism and 20th century Chinese Literatures, in The Reception and Rendition of Freud in China: China's Freudian Slip, (ed.) Tao Jiang, Philip J. Ivanhoe, Routledge, First Published, 2013, p.8

attempted at interpretation by explaining his own methodology, he writes: "There are two angles from which we could attempt to reach an understanding of this history of a case of paranoia and to lay bare in it the familiar complexes and motive forces of mental life. We might start either from the patient's own delusional utterances or from the exciting causes of his illness."[336] As any artist would have chosen for its creative potentialities, Lu Xun prefers the former method in this story by concentrating the patient's own delusional utterances recorded in his diary. First entry of the diary sets the tone:

Tonight the moon is very bright.

I have not seen it for over thirty years, so today when I saw it I felt in unusually high spirits. I begin to realize that during the past thirty-odd years I have been in the dark; but now I must be extremely careful. Otherwise why should that dog at the Chao house have looked at me twice?

I have reason for my fear.[337]

The reason he found and noted in his third entry of the diary as

They eat human beings, so they may eat me.[338]

I too am a man, and they want to eat me![339]

Rest of the entries in diary revolves around his fear and phobia to become victim of cannibalism. In one of the longest entry in his diary, he writes

---

336 Sigmund Freud, Case Histories II, The Pelican Freud Library, Vol.9, Penguin Books, 1979, p168

337 A Madman's Diary in *Selected Stories of Lu Xun, ibid, p.27*

338 Ibid, p.28

339 Ibid, p.29

"In ancient times, as I recollect, people often ate human beings, but I am rather hazy about it. I tried to look this up, but my history has no chronology, and scrawled all over each page are the words: "Virtue and Morality." Since I could not sleep anyway, I read intently half the night, until I began to see words between the lines, the whole book being filled with the two words—"Eat people."[340]

The diary-writer summarizes the history of Chinese civilization in two words, "eat people", and he substantiates it with some well known examples from Chinese history: According to ancient records, Yi Ya cooked his son and presented him to Duke Huan of Chi who reigned from 685 to 643 B.C. Chieh and Chou were tyrants of an earlier age. A revolutionary at the end of the Ching dynasty (1644-1911), Hsu Hsi-lin was executed in 1907 for assassinating a Ching official. His heart and liver were eaten. In ancient times Yi Ya boiled his son for Chieh and Chou to eat; that is the old story. But actually since the creation of heaven and earth by Pan Ku men have been eating each other, from the time of Yi Ya's son to the time of Hsu Hsi-lin and from the time of Hsu Hsi-lin down to the man caught in Wolf Cub Village. Last year they executed a criminal in the city, and a consumptive soaked a piece of bread in his blood and sucked it.

Key Ray Chong, in his work *Cannibalism in China* opines that as far as practicing *survival cannibalism* is concerned, the Chinese are not especially different from other cultures but, they are utterly unique in their use of so-called "learned cannibalism". Learned cannibalism is quite the opposite of its survival-orientated counterpart, and is widely considered to be "an expression of love and hatred, and a peculiar extension of Confucian doctrine."[341]Madman criticizes in

340 Ibid

341 Key Ray Chong, *Cannibalism in China*. Hollow brook Publishing, 1990

his diary the Confucian filial piety, what is eulogized in tradition by the respect and loyalty of a child shown to a parent. *Virtue and Morality* are elusive words that *scrawled all over the page* of Chinese history to hide Confucian hierarchies, patriarchy, nepotism, pure inequality, and moral dictatorship.

In one place diary-writer discusses this matter with his elder brother in these words: *"Brother, probably all primitive people ate a little human flesh to begin with. Later, because their outlook changed, some of them stopped, and because they tried to be good they changed into men, changed into real men. But some are still eating—just like reptiles. Some have changed into fish, birds, monkeys and finally men; but some do not try to be good and remain reptiles still. When those who eat men compare themselves with those who do not, how ashamed they must be. Probably much more ashamed than the reptiles are before monkeys."*[342]

This is a provocative piece of arguments where evolution of cannibalism is outlined and Social Darwinism[343] is refuted —It is not the *natural selection* or the *survival of the fittest* that drives the wheel of evolution move forward but the urge to *try to be good*. Now this story becomes an allegory that touches the realm of parable as Story ends with the motto: *"Perhaps there are still children who have not eaten men? Save the children. . . "* If cannibalism is psychopathology of social Darwinism, then to *save the children* would be saving the future from the madness of civilization. Civilization that promotes cannibalism, literal as well

---

(https://en.wikipedia.org/wiki/Cannibalism in China; accessed on 2.10.2018)

342 A Madman's Diary, *Ibid, p.34*

343 *"Social Darwinism is that enterprise or ideology founded in the nineteenth century, which holds social evolution to depend upon the operation of the law of natural selection of favorable veritable variants."* R.J.Haliday, Victorian Studies, vol.14, No.4,(June 1971), p.389

as metaphorically as *big fishes eat small ones*; it is clearly another form of madness. Michel Foucault (1926 – 1984) begins his preface of *Madness and Civilization* with these quotations: *"Men are so necessarily mad, that not to be mad would amount to another form of madness."*(Pascal) *And "It is not by confining one's neighbor that one is convinced of one's own sanity."*[344](Dostoievsky) Like two powerful headlights, it throws light on the dark and misty trajectories of madness in the path of civilization.

The question, that is pertinent to ask is, could we perceive madness and civilization in a binary opposite way or we look beyond this differentiation as Foucault has recommended in his insightful work *Madness and Civilization: "We must try to return, in history, to that zero point in the course of madness at which madness is an undifferentiated experience, a not yet divided experience of division itself. We must describe, from the start of its trajectory, that "other form" which relegates Reason and Madness to one side or the other of its action as things henceforth external, deaf to all exchange, and as though dead to one another."*[345]

The diary-writer observes the madness in civilization as people in civilization sees madness in him; like a two way mirror positioned between them, this story does not try to *relegate Reason and Madness to one side or the other* and this is the crux and brilliance of the story, showing the ugliness of differentiated experiences of madness and sanity.

---

344 See this episode of the story: *Old Chen hurried forward and dragged me home. He dragged me home. The folk at home all pretended not to know me; they had the same look in their eyes as all the others. When I went into the study, they locked the door outside as if cooping up a chicken or a duck.*

345 Foucault, Michel, ibid, p.9

Lu Xun's *The True Story of Ah Q*

The True Story of Ah Q is the most famous fictional work[346] of Lu Xun(1881-1936), written in the culmination of the Chinese Vernacular Revolution, first published serially[347] and later included in his first short story collection *Call to Arms* (Nahan) in 1923. Though technically speaking it is like a novella since it contains 42 pages, shorter than full length novels but it is divided in chapters and quite longer than usual short stories. A notable structural feature of this work is the preface or prologue as Introduction in the story that starts with following lines: *For several years now I have been meaning to write the true story of Ah Q. But while wanting to write I was in some trepidation, too, which goes to show that I am not one of those who achieve glory by writing; for an immortal pen has always been required to record the deeds of an immortal man, the*

346 "By virtue of more than sixty reprinting and translation into more than thirty languages, numerous dramatic performances, production as a film and ballet, and depictions in cartoon and woodcut form (Peng 1993: 420, 546-548), "True Story" can be counted as Lu Xun's most famous work. An immense volume of commentary on the work has developed since its earliest critical reception in the Chinese literary world. These works form a category within Lu Xun studies generally called "Ah Q Research" (Ah Q yanjiu).I refer to the critical body of work and the various interpretations and reinterpretations as the "Ah Q discourse." The Ironic Inflation of Chinese National Character: Lu Xun's International Reputation, Romain Rolland's Critique of "The True Story of Ah Q," and the Nobel Prize, Paul B. Foster, Modern Chinese Literature and Culture, Spring, 2001, Vol. 13, No. 1, pp. 144

347 First published serially in nine issues over a two-month period from 4th December 1921 to 12th February 1922 and that in a weekly supplement of a news paper Peking ch'en Pao(Morning Post) for its column titled K'ai-hsin Hua(Cheerful Anecdotes) but soon its inappropriateness for this column was realized by the author and editor so it was moved to another section of the paper called "New Literature"

man becoming known to posterity through the writing and the writing known to posterity through the man - until finally it is not clear who is making whom known. But in the end, as though possessed by some fiend, I always came back to the idea of writing the story of Ah Q.[348] Generally Fiction is defined as *a* literature *created from the imagination, not presented as fact, though it may be based on a true story or situation*[349] but here the narrator wants to present his story as facts. In fact, some critics have been surprised by this introduction, while others simply overlooked its structural importance. Commenting its link with traditional Chinese fiction, William Lyell writes: *he spends a good deal of his introduction on a rambling digression in which he takes pot shots at a number of favorite enemies before getting into the story proper. Were he actually to tell the tale in a teashop, this device would serve as a good filler waiting for customers to come in; one could even enter the shop as he began on Installment II and still get one's money's worth, losing very little of the story proper. Perhaps, in consenting to write such a serial in the first place, Lu Xun was intrigued by the scope it would afford him to experiment with the techniques of traditional Chinese fiction....And of course, given the serial nature of the story, we cannot logically expect it to be characterized by scene economy.*[350] Here it is clear that for Lyell introduction is not integral part of the *story proper* and it is simply a *rambling digression* but if we see the whole structure of the story in totality doesn't it appear that the introduction is a device to make reader aware about its becoming, it's self-reflexivity? Is it not a device for inviting the reader to see the

---

348 The True Story of Ah Q, Yang Hsien-yi & Gladys Yang (Tr.), Foreign Languages Press, Peking, 1953, p.1

349 https://www.britannica.com/art/fiction-literature (accessed on 31/12/2020)

350 Lyell, William, Jr., Lu Hsun's Vision of Reality, Univ. of California Press,, Berkeley, pp. 286-287

process of becoming? It looks like an example of Asian performance and theatre tradition where it makes less of an attempt to hide the "performance" aspect of the work. They try their best to show their awareness that they're performing, and the audience isn't there to get "lost in the moment."[351] Bertold Brecht noted after watching Mei Lanfang (1894-1961), a Chinese performance in Moscow in March 1935, he writes: *Traditional Chinese acting also knows the alienation effect, and applies it most subtly....Chinese artist never act as if there were a fourth wall besides the three surrounding him. He expresses his awareness of being watched*[352].similarly, this introduction, it seems is meant to generate same kind of alienation- effect by discussing elaborately about various possible forms or genres suitable for his subject directly and intimately addressing to the readers: *And yet no sooner had I taken up my pen than I became conscious of tremendous difficulties in writing this far-from immortal work. The first was the question of what to call it. Confucius said, "If the name is not correct, the words will not ring true"; and this axiom should be most scrupulously observed. There are many types of biographies: official\ biographies, autobiographies, unauthorized biographies, legends, supplementary biographies, family histories, sketches but unfortunately none of these suited my purpose*[353]....these are the genres /forms narrator discusses in the introduction, one by one, judging its suitability for the

---

351 **"***Lu Xun, however, begins the "story" not by establishing the probability of a biography, but by throwing it into irredeemable awkwardness, to the extent that the subject of this self-claimed biographical project becomes so uncertain and obscure that no story can be meaningfully told at all.***"** Xuedong Zhang, The Will to Allegory and the Origin of Chinese Modernism: Rereading Lu Xun's *Ah Q—The Real Story in* The Oxford Handbook of Global Modernisms, Edited by Mark Wollaeger and Matt Eatough, Oxford University Press, 2018.p.9

352 Brecht, Bertold. "Alienation Effects in Chinese Acting". Willett, John (ed. and trans.). *Brecht on Theatre***.** Eyre Methuen, London, 2001.pp.91-92

353 The True Story of Ah Q, ibid

proposed subject (Ah Q) as well his own capability or incapability to do so; Here he sounds like a well-informed critic, who is putting his case in front of his possible reading public and this is what makes this work like a metafiction, which deals with writing and its own composition in a self-conscious manner. Mark curry defined *meta fiction as a borderline discourse, as a kind of writing which places itself on the border between fiction and criticism, and which takes that border as its subject....The writer / critic is thus a dialectical figure, embodying both the production and reception of fiction in the roles of author and reader in a way that is paradigmatic for metafiction.*[354] What is true for *alienation* in performances, borderline discourse does the same with fiction.

The writer/critic's borderline discourse on proposed genres for his subject Ah Q starts with official biography and it does not suit his subject as *What place could the life of the miserable Ah-Q have next to the glorious, official biographies of the rich and famous installed in our hallowed court histories?*[355] Obviously this statement throws ample light on his subject at the same time on his own (narrator's) intellectualscape, his ability in critiquing the genre of official biography as such. It reminds us the subaltern critique of elite historiography.[356] Though some of the critics has emphasized it as a conventional means to elevate this narrative: "*While traditional*

---

354 Metafiction, Mark Currie (Edited and Introduced), Routledge, 2013, pp.2-3

355 The Real Story of A –Q, Julia Lovell(tr.), Penguin Books, 2009

356 "*For parallel to the domain of elite politics there existed throughout the colonial period another domain of Indian politics in which the principal actors were not the dominant groups of the indigenous society or the colonial authorities but the subaltern classes and groups constituting the mass of the laboring population and the intermediate strata in town and country—that is, the people.* " Ranjit Guha, On Some Aspects of the Historiography of Colonial India, Subaltern Studies I, OUP, Delhi, 1982, p.4

historiography (including the subgenre biography, liezhuan) is always in "elegant discourse" (Wenyan), during the Ming and Qing periods fiction in the vernacular could take as its protagonist a person of any social class. Authors of Ming and Qing novels and stories often referred to the imputed parallels between historiography and their work to enhance the verisimilitude of the latter. Ironically, for this "modern" story, the narrator alludes to this conventional means of authentication to "elevate" his narrative."[357] Certainly this is not the case if we don't take whole introduction as author' statement about his work. It is about a character and characterization.

Second choice of genre, he discusses is autobiography it can't be autobiography if we take the whole exercise of this introduction is to establish objective distance with the subject and it goes without saying that he is not Ah Q. After second choice there are some variations in order and explanation in different English translations of this work that underline not only the problem of cross-cultural translation but the culture specific origin and evolution of genres across history. For example discussing about probability of presenting the story of Ah Q as *Mythological record* or *Histories of the relatives of the emperor's wives,* translation A gives the following explanation, "*If this is to be called an outside record where is his inside record? If the title mythological record is used, it is clear that Ah Q is not a supernatural being. Here we have a play on Chinese characters. The two characters wai-ch'uan separately mean "outside" and "record" but taken together mean a record of the wives of the emperor's relations. Here the character wai is played against the character nei, which is to follow and which means "inside"; but again the play goes on with a subtle turn because the phrase, nei-chuan literally "inside record:" used*

357 Martin Weizong Huang, The Inescapable Predicament: The Narrator and His Discourse in "The True Story of Ah Q", Modern China, Oct., 1990, Vol. 16, No. 4 (Oct., 1990), p.447 note13

together means a mythological record. Whereas translation b and c puts it under the genre *legends* and gives only one line explanation: *The use of "legend' is impossible, because Ah Q was no legendary figure* (Trans. B): *If I were to call my account the stuff of legend, it could legitimately be objected that Ah-Q is no god* (Trans.C).It is very evident in these descriptions that Trans. B and C not only tries to overlook the play of Chinese characters and context of its speech acts[358] but simply ignores the specificity of a particular genre in a particular culture as Todorov has rightly emphasized that *Genres communicate indirectly with the society where they are operative through their institutionalization. Each epoch has its own system of genres, which stands in some relation to the dominant ideology, and so on. Like any other institution, genres bring to light the constitutive features of the society to which they belong...a society chooses and codifies the acts that correspond most closely to its ideology; that is why the existence of certain genres in one society, their absence in another, are revelatory of that ideology and allows to establish it more or less confidently. It is not a coincidence that the epic is possible in one period, the novel in another, with the individual hero of the novel opposed to the collective hero of the epic: each of these choices depends upon the ideological framework within which it operates."*[359]In a society where Biography is not a part of Historiography, Special Biography, Supplementary Biography, and Unauthorized Biography——three names for the

358 In the philosophy of language and linguistics, speech act is something expressed by an individual that not only presents information, but performs an action too. It is an utterance defined in terms of a speaker's intention and the effect it has on a listener. Essentially, it is the action that the speaker hopes to provoke in his or her audience. Speech acts might be requests, warnings, promises, apologies, greetings, or any number of declarations. See, J. L. Austin, How to Do Things With Words, OUP, 1962

359 Tzvetan Todorov, The Origin of Genres in Modern Genre Theory, David Duff (ed.) Routledge, 2000, p.200

same thing in three translations show the inadequacy of particular genre in target language but at the same time, it is puzzling to read the explanation, writer gives, "*To 'unauthorized biography', I gave some thought: but where is the authorized version? No president has ever ordered his National Institute of Historical Research to create such a memorial to Ah-Q. True, our revered translators have rendered the great Conan Doyle's Rodney Stone as Unauthorized Biographies of the Gamblers – though I am willing to bet no official counterpart exists in Britain's National Archive. But while men of literary genius can take such license, I have no comparable entitlement.*" This declaration, more than inadequacy of a sub-genre, raises few questions about the discourse behind such argument. *Rodney Stone (1896)* is a work of fiction and its author Sir Arthur Conan Doyle (1859-1930) has never claimed that it is an *Unauthorized Biographies of the Gamblers* and that was rendered only in Chinese translation by revered Chinese translators so it is ambiguous to elaborate by saying that it has no official counterpart in Britain's National Archive, further the question of entitlement becomes redundant. And finally the conclusion where narrator says, "*This effort of mine, I can only conclude, is the standard, official biography of the man; and yet the debased vulgarity of its content and characters causes me to shy, appalled, from such presumption. So at last, I will fall back on the formulation so often used by our nation's novelists –the very dregs of our glorious literary tradition – in their constant battle with digression: 'Now back to the real story.' There: The Real Story of Ah-Q it is. Any similarity between the present work and the unforgettable Real Story of Calligraphy, by Mr. Feng Wu of the Qing dynasty, is entirely unintentional.*"[360]so the circle is complete in the conclusion —- Here two things are made interrelated —- first the narrator's final solution for his quest

360 Julia Lovell(tr.), The Real Story of A Q, Penguin Books, 2009

to find proper title and genre for his subject and second, some justification or rationale for his own so-called digression for reaching to this conclusion.Now, back to the true story, which raises the question of whether the prologue is a fictional tale designed to achieve a voluntary suspension of disbelief[361] or whether it is a metanarrative, a genre of fiction in which the process of creation of the work becomes the subject of the work, thereby breaking the shackles of realism; *The true story of Ah Q* elaborates this point further—- remember the final scene of the execution of Ah Q:

"Help, help!"

But Ah Q never uttered these words. All had turned black before his eyes, there was a buzzing in his ears, and he felt as if his whole body were being scattered like so much light dust.[362]

Jeremy Tambling comments: *"The text has required the narrator to say something that he cannot know (he cannot know that Ah Q tried to say 'Help') and that impossibility sorts with another, that the reader is asked to enter the experience of a man who dies and is dead, becoming a body in pieces (corps morcele), the fantasy that the psychoanalyst Jacques Lacan (1900-1981) discusses, of being fragmented, perhaps torn to pieces. It is as though there can be an experience of being dead."*[363] Was it possible in a realistic way to expose the limits of perceived reality and its transgression before the reader? Lu Shun always got a 'no' answer to this question; no wonder his stories like The

361 *"...to transfer from our inward nature a human interest and a semblance of truth sufficient to procure for these shadows of imagination that willing suspension of disbelief for the moment, which constitutes poetic faith."* S.T. Coleridge, Biographia Literaria, *Chapter XIV*

362 Julia Lovell(tr.), ibid, p.152

363 Jeremy Tambling, Madmen and other survivors, Reading Lu Xun's Fiction, Hong Kong University Press, Aberdeem, Hong kong, 2007, p.9

Unique Sword and Flight to the Moon remind us of Latin American magical realism. Read this passage of *Forging the swords: Twenty years ago, the king's concubine gave birth to a piece of iron which they said she conceived after embracing an iron pillar. It was pure, transparent iron. The king, realizing that this was a rare treasure, decided to have it made into a sword with which to defend his kingdom, kill his enemies and ensure his own safety, As ill luck would have it, your father was chosen for the task, and in both hands he brought the iron home. He tempered it day and night for three whole years, until he had forged two swords.*[364]

How this inexplicable event in the story can be understood especially when writer depicts it in very matter of factly fashion. Guatemalan author William Spindler's article, "Magic realism: a typology," suggests that there are three kinds of magic realism, which however are by no means incompatible: European 'metaphysical' magic realism, with its sense of estrangement and the uncanny, exemplified by Kafka's fiction; 'ontological' magical realism, characterized by 'matter-of-factness' in relating 'inexplicable' events; and 'anthropological' magical realism, where a Native worldview is set side by side with the Western rational worldview.[365] It can be safely argued that while *Forging the sword* can be categorized 'ontological'; The flight to the moon or Medicine may be called 'anthropological'. In both these stories a kind of medicine —-that was traditionally believed in the society was made cornerstone of the plot and Lu Xun concludes its after-effect without being harsh or sounding anti-traditional. In *Medicine* son dies even after giving him bread with fresh blood of a decapitated

364 Forging the Sword, Lu Xun selected works, ibid, p.298

365 William Spindler, Magic realism: a typology, Forum for Modern Language Studies. (1993) Vol. xxxix No. 1, pp. 75-85

boy[366] and in *The flight to the moon* protagonist, believing that her wife must have taken the flight to the moon after consuming elixir; informs coolly in the last paragraph: "*Tomorrow I am going to ask that priest for another elixir, so that I can follow her.*"[367] Fiction writer Lu Xun deconstructs here, a particular world-view by not demolishing it realistically rather putting it as construct of a belief system and its trappings and its fatal consequences.

Noted Hindi writer Gajanan Madhav Muktibodh, reviewing a collection of Lu Xun's short stories in 1954 comments about the story Medicine in following words:

"The theatricality in the story Medicine is splendid—- this is the reason why the deep melancholy of the story does not hurt so much. It is full of symbolism and psychology. This is a story of execution of a revolutionary leader in the midst of bewildered masses, where depiction of masses is of prime importance. And the end of the story is really grand.

"*Two mothers met in a crematorium. Both had buried their children here. This is dawn and there is loneliness all over. The son of a mother had sacrificed his life for the country while other mother's son could not be saved from tuberculosis even after giving him a small dose of live blood. Diseased son and revolutionary son —both had lost their life in the same social condition. The same society had created both but turned them too against each other. And then both mothers return, looking the crow flying towards horizon from the crematorium. In their folk tales, crow is symbol of soul and women's companion and horizon symbolizes future.*"[368]

---

366 Medicine, Lu Xun selected works, ibid, pp.58-67.

367 The flight to the moon, Lu Xun selected works, ibid, p.295

368 Nemichandra Jain(ed.), Muktibodh rachnavali, vol.5, Rajkamal Paperbacks, Delhi, First edition, 1985, p.411

Muktibodh is a committed writer and famous for his fantasies and symbolism in Hindi literature. No wonder he praises Lu Xun in no unequal terms and calls him 'the Valmiki of china's new age'.[369] Though Muktibodh is primarily a poet but his stories do supplement his poems —— the persona and the voice of the author is distinctly recognizable all through his writings. His fantasies create reality in non-real forms and his stories like *Claude Eatherly* and *The disciple of Brahmarakchasa* can be cited here as two great examples of this category. The story *Claude Eatherly* develops through dialogues between two strangers, one of them is a C.I.D informer and the other is a writer who is narrating the story. The narrator does not know that just a minute before with whom he got an eye contact, just out of curiosity to look what is inside in a mysterious building of a mental asylum is famous Claude Eatherly. After knowing it from the informer, irritatingly he asks then, "Is it not Hindustan then? Are we living in America?

He guffawed over my foolishness and said, "There is America in each big city of Hindustan. Did not you see white golden women with red bright lips and their costly attires? Did not you notice overeducated gentry roaming around in luxurious cars? Did not you find a kind of sophisticated adultery? Did not you see seminars? Once upon a time we used to go to London and called 'London returned' and today we go to Washington. Given a chance and if we become equally rich then nothing will be as good as having equal number of atom bombs, hydrogen bombs and rockets."[370]

Historical Claude Robert Eatherly (1918 - 1978) was an officer in the U.S. Army Air Forces during World War II. He was the weather

---

369 ibid, p.412.

370 ibid, vol.3, pp.157-158

pilot who reported and gave green signal for the dropping of the atomic bomb on Hiroshima, Japan, August 6, 1945. Years later, Eatherly claimed to have become horrified for his participation in the Hiroshima bombing. He tried speaking out with pacifist groups (especially with Gunther Anders, a Viennese philosopher and pacifist), sending monetary helps to Hiroshima, writing letters of apology, and once or twice attempted suicide. But some contrary facts about him are also prevalent, Jerome Klinkowitz writes in 'American Flyers in World War II': "Shortly after leaving the Air Force in 1947, Eatherly took part in arrangements for a raid on Cuba by American adventurers hoping to overthrow the government; here the former weather pilot's responsibilities would involve a flight of bomb-laden P-38 Lightning obtained as war surplus. The plot was uncovered, and Eatherly was arrested and prosecuted, serving time in jail for this offense."[371]

Claude Eatherly was a controversial person but Muktibodh made him a symbol of conscience and compassion. CID informer tells the author in the story that, who does not know that Claude Eatherly is a voice of the soul that opposes nuclear war. Eatherly is not a mental patient. He is a symbol of spiritual conflicts and unrest. And later in the story when narrator refutes his claim that India is America he says that difficulty with you is that you don't understand my intents and then he clarifies Claude Eatherly may not exist in his bodily form here but restless souls like him might exist. And later after some deliberations he proves that the people like you who are conscious sensitive are Claude Eatherly.[372] Claude Etherly's story becomes the story of contemporary relevance of a

371 http://en.wikipedia.org/wiki/Claude_Eatherly(accessed on 4.11.2012)

372 Nemichandra Jain(ed.), Muktibodh rachnavali, vol.3, Rajkamal Paperbacks, Delhi, p.161

conscious, aware and sensitive being and this contemporaneity is also visible in its presentation.

Like this story, the *Disciple of Brahmarakchasa* is also set against the backdrop of mystery. Brahmarakshas's question of moral responsibility inherent in the disciple's acquisition of knowledge has been presented through a mysterious moral tale. Here, the discourse of knowledge that Muktibodh wants to put forward is different from Foucault's discourse of knowledge/power[373]. While for Foucault the essence of knowledge is power, for Muktibodh the essence of knowledge is in its dissemination, which, if stopped, makes a man Brahmarakchasa, despite not being in a condition like Foucault's discipline *and punishment*[374]. The opening lines of this story set the tone: *The disciple's face radiated with some inner light as he alighted from eighth floor to seventh floor's lonely steps of that majestic building. He was not impressed by the miracle that he had just witnessed. That huge thunderous iron-arm crossing an entire length of three rooms kept flashing again and again in front of his eyes. The sacredness of that arm mattered to him but not as a miracle. There was 'something' behind that miracle that is churning him continuously. Is it not that- 'that something'- contains the truth of a great scholar's life?*

---

373 "the exercise of power itself creates and causes to emerge new objects of knowledge and accumulates new bodies of information...the exercise of power perpetually creates knowledge and conversely knowledge constantly induces effects of power." Colin Gordon, Colin Gordon (ed.) Power/ Knowledge Selected interviews and other writings, Michel Foucault, Pantheon Books, New york, 1980, pp.51-52

374 "The creation of a tamed body through surveillance and control that can be easily controlled and that, through training, can reach a state of self-control." Discipline and Punish: The Birth of the Prison, Vintage Books, New York, 1979, p. 135

Yes, it is! It definitely is!![375] And then the story goes into flashback to when that 'miracle' happened and the truth about Mahapandit's life was revealed.

In Hindu mythology, Brahmarakchasas are considered to be fierce demon spirits. It is actually the spirit of a Brahmin, a dead scholar of high birth, who has done evil things in his life or has misused his knowledge, so he has to suffer as a Brahmarakchasa after his or her death. If he wants liberation from this he has to find an able disciple who can impart his great knowledge, otherwise he would remain Brahmarakchasa forever. As Lu Xun turned china's old traditional tales into stories of contemporary sensibilities, Muktibodh turns this myth into a story of moral responsibility that knowledge or wisdom inheres. Brahmarakchasa proclaims to his disciple in the story that *"I have churned all the knowledge of the world but unfortunately could not find any suitable disciple to dissipate/disseminate it to him or her. This is the reason my soul remained attached to this world and I as a Brahmarakchasa remained here. ... and then you came...by receiving my wisdom you liberated me. I have fulfilled my responsibilities that wisdom inheres. Now my responsibility is all yours and until you impart my given wisdom to someone else you can't be liberated.* "[376] It is worth noting here that the Guru here demands only the dissemination of knowledge and affection from the disciple; he neither demands loyalty nor allegiance nor insistence on limiting knowledge to himself or his sect, but by his own example warns him of the danger of doing so. This role of the Guru is completely different from that of the Upanishadic or devotional Guru.

---

375 Nemichandra Jain(ed.), Muktibodh rachnavali, vol.3, Rajkamal Paperbacks, Delhi, p.114

376 Ibid, p.119-20

In the European Enlightenment, knowledge was understood as a form of rational functionalism, where it was appreciated as a means of mastering and using the world. Such an approach implied hostility towards any form of mystery. As Adorno and Horkheimer[377] argue, realistic fiction, steeped in rational functionalism, naturalizes the world as a familiar, morally and socially graded and predictable object. But why does much of Lu Xun and Muktibodh's fiction not allow the world to become 'naturalized as a familiar, morally and socially graded and predictable object', but rather questions it? They look at this world, the conditions of living in it, its rituals, its known and unknown aspects, from an angle from which the veils of everyday understanding begin to lift and what is unknown never becomes a cause of fear.

377 Theodor Adorno and Max Horkheimer, Dialectics of Enlightenment, Verso, London, 1994, p.42

14

The Reception of Hispanic Literature in Hindi

There could be two ways to look or analyze the reception of any particular literature or text in any given language— one is to trace the history of reception (knowing fully well the problematic of History-writing of any kind) and the other is to ascertain the motives and patronage behind any translation. Most of the time motives and patronage are interlinked and as Russian Formalists have shown, the base of the linkages could be ideological, Economic or status related[378] The history of reception of Hispanic literature in Hindi starts with the translation of Cervantes's Don Quixote— first it appeared in 1926 (as Vichitra Vir from Ganga Pustak mala karyalaya, Lucknow) and then in 1958 another translation came (as Tismar Khan, Tr. By Shreekant Vyasa, Rajpal & sons, Delhi), next year another translation appeared (as Don Quixote ki Vichitra kathayen, Tr.By virendra mandal 'virendra', Subhash Pustak Mandir, Varanasi, 1959) and consequently in 1964 the most acclaimed translation of Chavinath Pandey came out from Sahitya Akademi as Don Quixote. All these translation were done through English so these were the translations of translation. Next important translation and to some extent a milestone in the field

378 Cited in Andre lefevere, Translation, Rewriting & the Manipulation of Literary Fame, Routledge London &New York, First Published 1992, pp.14-16

of Hispanic literature in Hindi, can be found in an anthology of translated poems of 1960 called *Deshantar*[379]; edited and translated by one of the major voices of Hindi literature: Dharamveer Bharati. In this celebrated anthology of world poetry Out of 160 total poems, 66 were chosen from Hispanic world: 57 from Latin America and 9 from Spain (table A):

(Table A)

Country	No. of Poet	No. of Poems
Spain	07	09
Argentina	08	09
Ecuador	01	04
Cuba	02	04
Costa Rica	03	03
Chile	04	07
Puerto rico	02	03
Peru	07	07
Brazil	05	08
Mexico	07	08
Venezuela	03	04
Total : 11	49	66

But this anthology that soon became a kind of modern classic of Hindi translation was also done through English. However the change came in 1969 when Premlata Verma translated some poems of Peruvian poet Cesar Vallejo (1892-1938) from the collection of *Los Heraldos Negros* directly from original Spanish[380]. Later she also translated epic poem *Martín Fierro* of Argentinean José Hernandez

379 Deshantar, ed.&tr.Dharamveer Bharati, Bhartiya Jnanpith, Punarnava edition, Delhi, 2003

380 Indian Art Press, Kailash Colony, Delhi.

(1834 – 1886).[381] But real difference, as far as Hindi translations of Hispanic literature is concerned, was made when a newly established university JNU (1969) had set up a full-fledged centre for teaching Spanish in 1971.Soon this centre had produced some of the most efficient translators in this field who later engaged in so many endeavors in importing Spanish works into Hindi: see Table (B).

(Table B)

Translators	Translated works	
	Iberian	Latin-American
Prabhati Nautiyal	Francisco De Quevedo, Buscón Ki Jeevan-Katha(1985), Vasco da Gama Ki Pahali Samudri Yatra Ka Rojanamacha (2000)	José Martí, José Martí Ki Kuchha Kavitayen(1976) Pablo Neruda, Ruko O Prithvi(1996) Juan Manuel Marcos, winter of Günter(2012)
Sonya Surabhi Gupta	Camilo José Cela, Pascual Duarte ka Parivaar,(1991), José Ortega y Gasset, Jansamuhon ka Vidroh, (1998),	Gabriel Garcia Marquez, Ekant ke Sau Varsh, (2003), Jorge Luis Borges, Chaku, Aine aur Bhulbhullaia, (2000), Carlos Fuentes, Chac Mool, 1996,
Aparajit Chattopadhyay (with Suresh Dhingra)	Pedro Calderon de la Barca,, salameya ka Sarpanch, 2003.	Ernesto Sabato, Surang (2009) Columbia ki kahaniyaan (ed). Gabriela Mistral, Tichar Didi Ki Matribhasha(2012)

381 Sahitya Akademi, New Delhi

Translators	Translated works	
	Iberian	Latin-American
S.P.Ganuly, Meenakshi Sundriyal, Kundan Kanan	Raphael Alberti, Dharati Ka Farishta(2004)	...Yah Sampannata Bikhari Huyee(2006)
Meenakshi Sundriyal, Alka Jaspal, Rama Paul		Poems of Gabriela Mistral, Rosario, Juana Delbarbourou, Castellano, Alfonsino Storni, DelmiraAgustini, Giconda Belli (2007)
Alka Jaspal, Anil Dhingra,	Poetes de les Illes Balears	
Arushie Jain, Kundan Kanan	Antologia Poetica (Poems of Antonio Machado, Juan Ramon Jimenez. Federico Garcia Lorca, Miguel Hernandez), 2005	
Ankita Rajkumar	Ana Maria Matute	

Though Delhi University was the first university in India in introducing Spanish language teaching in early sixties of last century but initially it was part-time one year certificate course ;it is only recently in 2002 that B.A.course and in 1988 that M.A.course was introduced. However some important and major works of Hispanic world were translated in Hindi by the associates of Department of Germanic and Romance Languages, University of Delhi: see Table(c). This table demonstrates few facts: first of all, poetry and fiction and to some extant plays were thought to be fit for the target literature and secondly Latin American literature[382] got huge prominence over Spanish literature: The ratio in Poetry is almost 1:10. Let us see what influences the translator or makes him to choose a particular text for translation. Dharamveer Bharati proclaims in the introduction of 'Deshantar': "whenever two cultural streams meet translation always been the useful medium of communication. But in modern context for a new poet poetry-translation has some other significance too. What is the reason everyone from Ezra Pound to Boris Pasternak tried to be engaged with translation-work.

382 "The remarkably vast and diverse domain of the literatures of Latin America does not lend itself to easy overviews.Nonethless, it; it is possible to identify a variety of criss-crossing movements, tropes and categories that link the literary production of the region (Mexico, Central America, Hispanic Caribbean islands, South America, including Portuguese- speaking Brazil)." Elzbieta Sklodowska, Latin American Literatures in The Companion to Latin American Studies, ed. Philip Swanson, Arnold publishers, London, 2003, P.87.

Translators	Translated works	
	Iberian	Latin-American
Vibha Maurya	Miguel de Cervantes Saavedra, Don Quijote: La Mancha ke Shoorvir ki Gatha-- Pratham Bhag, 2006. Javier Marias, Oxford ke Prani, 2003. Juan Benet, Vapas Rekhion ko, 2001. José Saramago, Lisbon ki Gherabandi ka Itihas, 1999-2000.	G. G. Marquez, Main Kiraye par Sapne Dekhti Hoon (Story) 1993. Juan Rulfo, Díles que no nos maten (Story), 1983. Rosario Castellano, Poems, Hans, 1988
Sabyasachi Mishra	Miguel de Cervantes Saavedra, Cervantes ke Udaharanatmak Upanyas, 2009	
Maneesha Taneja	Merce Rodoreda, Toota Aaaina, 2007 (With Vijaya Venkataraman)	Pablo Neruda, Haan maine zindagi jee hai, 2007
Meena Thakur, Anamika Kumari	Antologia Poetica (Poems of Antonio Machado, Juan Ramon Jimenez. Federico Garcia Lorca, Miguel Hernandez), 2005	

(Contd.)

Translators	Translated works	
	Iberian	Latin-American
Vibha Maurya	Miguel de Cervantes Saavedra, Don Quijote: La Mancha ke Shoorvir ki Gatha-- Pratham Bhag, 2006. Javier Marias, Oxford ke Prani, 2003. Juan Benet, Vapas Rekhion ko, 2001. José Saramago, Lisbon ki Gherabandi ka Itihas, 1999-2000.	G. G. Marquez, Main Kiraye par Sapne Dekhti Hoon (Story) 1993. Juan Rulfo, Díles que no nos maten (Story), 1983. Rosario Castellano, Poems, Hans, 1988
Sabyasachi Mishra	Miguel de Cervantes Saavedra, Cervantes ke Udaharanatmak Upanyas, 2009	
Maneesha Taneja	Merce Rodoreda, Toota Aaaina, 2007 (With Vijaya Venkataraman)	Pablo Neruda, Haan maine zindagi jee hai, 2007
Meena Thakur, Anamika Kumari	Antologia Poetica (Poems of Antonio Machado, Juan Ramon Jimenez. Federico Garcia Lorca, Miguel Hernandez), 2005	

"It has some special reason.

"The master-disciple tradition was an important and significant component of the poet's occupation in medieval period. Every budding poet used to accept some master-poet who has right to suggest or improve his works. According to his suggestion poet used to practice and when he is about to attain maturity he is in the verge of inventing and establishing his own individual style.

"But modern poetry that grew in a revolutionary mental state, the master-directed-disciplined -practicing -tradition not only became redundant but limiting and harmful too....but every budding poet (whether he admits or not) needs some direction, discipline and practice ...and if he does not agree with his immediate predecessor then he may select according to his nature from predecessors of his immediate predecessor so he can practice and immersed into it by translating it and in this way he enriches his expression."[383]

So here the motivating factor for translation is to enrich his own expression. This is highly subjective and poet-oriented approach—that can only be generalized, if we focus our attention to the creative process of translator rather than from the receptor's point of view. But other most important anthology of Latin –American & Caribbean poets (see Table E) ...*yeh Sampannata Bikhari Hui* gives different explanation: "Since the list of poets for our collection was provided mainly by the Delhi based Latin American and Caribbean embassies so understandably it was the symbol of their Cultural policies....this anthology not only brings sensibility of the original to poetry lovers without the intervention of English but it will also provide the useful reference material for literature and translation studies."[384]

---

383 Dharamveer Bharati, ibid, pp.7-8

384 ...yeh Sampannata Bikhari Hui, Ed & Tr. Shyama Prasad Ganguly, Meenakshi Sundriyal, Sahitya Akademi & Grulac, First Edition 2006, pp.29

8.Susnigdha Dey, Spanish Literature ; Aspects & Appraisal, B.R.Publishing Corporation, Delhi, 1991, p.130

(Table E)

Country	No of Poets	No. of Poems
Argentina	06	09
Brazil	05	09
Chile	08.	08
Colombia	05	05
Costa Rica	02	08
Cuba	05	07
Ecuador	03	03
Guyana	02	03
Mexico	08	08
Panama	05	09
Peru	02	07
Surinam	05	05
Trinidad & Tobago	05	05
Uruguay	08	08
Venezuela	02	09
Total :15	71	103

The role of foreign embassies in translating their national literature is of vital importance. Embassies all over the world promote and propagate their cultural treasure, but their activities differ as per their national policies. It is said that Brazilian literature is not being promoted here but other even very small countries of Latin-America have been very pro-active in India. It can be argued that the Third –world politics have also made Latin American literature more viable then Spanish mainland literature in India. IN 1991, one of the pioneers of Spanish Studies in India Prof.Susnigdha Dey announced quite prophetically that, "The emergence of the Third World is certainly a very important factor which will bring about far-reaching political, social and economic changes. There is a tendency among the developing nations of Latin America, to move closer to the policy of non-alignment. They are gradually coming out of the American orbit and taking their place in a world which is gradually emerging as freer than ever before from pressures blocks."[385]

It is a fact that should be highlighted here that Neruda and later Octavio Paz, Borges and Marquez became most popular amongst translators of post-colonial India. Putting things in context Brian Gollnick had rightly highlighted the fact that "In the first half of the twentieth century, Latin American literature was dominated by the region's poets, many of whom were active participants in the international avant-garde. Latin American narrative would not attain a similar international profile until the second half of the twentieth century, when a series of experimental novelists achieved recognition outside the region. This shift culminated in the 1960s with the 'Boom' of the Latin American novel, and the popularity of authors like Gabriel Garcia Marquez (Colombia), Carlos Fuentes (Mexico), Julio Cortazar (Argentina, 1914-84) and Mario Vargas Llosa (Peru) quickly eclipsed the poet's legacy."[386]

But in Hindi no one could eclipse Neruda as he alone attracted more then twenty five translators in Hindi that is in itself a record — no foreign writer had this luck of getting such a reception in Hindi. It is heartening to see that some of his translators are front ranking poet of Hindi like Shamsher Bahadur Singh, Dharmaveer Bharati, Shreekant Verma, Sarveshwar Dayal Saxena, Kedarnath Singh, Kamlesh, Vishnu Khare, and Arun Kamal.Though these poet-translators have done their translations through English but some full length anthologies were also done directly from

385 Brian Gollnick, Approaches to Latin-American Literature, in (ed.) Philip Swanson, ibid, p.108

386

Spanish original. The reception and popularity of Neruda in Hindi is baffling. Not only his poems were hugely popular amongst the translators but writers were never tired writing memoirs about him, poets were composing poems after reading his 'memoirs' and he also appeared in one of the most powerful poems of Hindi as 'truly lovable postman of the peace post-office of the world'[387] The question is how to understand this phenomenon — could we link the reflection in his oeuvre of a similar political-economy and ideology that connects the experience of Asia, Africa & Latin America or was it simply the aesthetic merit, devoid of any politics that were the only criterion for the popularity of his work in Hindi?

If we compare him with other Latin American poet of his time, like Octavio Paz (1914-1998), Jorge Luis Borges(1899-1986), Ernesto Cardinal (1925-) or for that matter with his own fellow countryman like of Gabriela Mistral (1889-1957) or Nicanor Parra (1914-) it would be difficult to understand his popularity on the ground of his aesthetic or ideological superiority.

In conclusion it can be said that to know and grasp the phenomenon of reception the study of history or the aesthetic and ideological base in isolation is not enough rather it requires an insight that can see how the dynamics of these entire three components make it work.

387 "मैं जोश की वह मस्ती हूँ जो नेरूदा की भवों से / जाम की तरह टकराती है/बह मेरा नेरूदा जो दुनिया के शांति पोस्ट आफिस का / प्यारा और सच्चा क़ासिद" अमन का राग, बात बोलेगी, शमशेर, सम्भावना प्रकाशन, हापुड़, प्रथम प्रकाशन, 1981, पृ.80

15

Post-Coloniality and Translation in Hindi

Just as fire can be fought by fire, textual control can be fought by textuality...The post-colonial is especially and pressingly concerned with the power that resides in discourse and textuality; its resistance, then, quite appropriately takes place in—and from—the domain of textuality, in (among other things) motivated acts of reading.[388]

Translation always involves a kind of motivated act of reading but the nature of motivation depends. When Bhartendu translated 'The Merchant of Venice' not only the title of the play but the name of characters, place and religion was domesticated. Now it is 'Durlabh Bandhu' and the place is not Venice but 'Vanshpur' and Shylock is not a Jew but a Jain, Shailaksh. And not only that, here is a scene when shylock comments on Antonio : "(Aside) How like a fawning publican he looks. I hate him for he is a Christian; / But more, for that in low simplicity/ He lends out money gratis and brings down/The rate of usance here with us in Venice."[389] And Bhartendu translates: "(आप ही आप) देखो इसकी सूरत से ही से यह बात झलकती है कि यह हिन्दुओं को प्रसन्न करने के लिए जैनियों से शत्रुता रखता है। मैं इससे घृणा करता हूँ क्योंकि यह ईसाई है

388 A. Lawson & Tiffin, Describing Empire: Post colonialism and Textuality, Rutledge, London, 1994, p.10

389 William Shakespeare, The Merchant of Venice, Macmillan India ltd., 2008, pp.35-36

परंतु मुख्यत: इस कारण से कि यह ऐसा निरुत्साह और नीच है कि लोगों को रुपया बिना व्याज के ऋण दे देकर हमलोगों के व्याज का भाव बिगाड़ देता है।"[390]

Here before the translation begins there is an interpolation: "see his very face reveals that he keeps animosity to Jains only to please the Hindus." It raises the obvious question why Bhartendu inserted it almost out of the blue: especially when Bhartendu does not replace Jew vs. Christian animosity to Jain vs. Hindu in the text, rather it is Jain vs. Christian that seems far-fetched if you keep the 'violent deal' of the play at hindsight. But later it becomes clear when Shailaksh addresses Anant (Christian Antonio) an Arya and Anant ridicules him by saying: "यह जैन ऐसा कृपालु होता जाता है कि आर्य बन जाएगा।"[391] ("The Hebrew will turn Christian; he grows kind"[392]). Now the question to be asked here is whether Bhartendu was emphasizing the Aryan theory of race—we can well remember Keshab Chandra Sen's words: "...in the advent of the English nation in India we see a reunion of parted cousins, the descendants of two different families of the ancient Aryan race..."[393] or was it a 'colonial mimicry' in the sense Bhabha uses it—'to subvert the master-discourse' : "....in the colonial context 'the English book'(the western text, whether religious like the Bible, or literary like Shakespeare) is made to symbolize English authority itself. But the process whereby a text or a book stands in for an entire culture is a complex, and ultimately fraught exercise. The process of replication is never complete or perfect, and what it produces is not simply a perfect image of the original but something changed because of the context in which it is being reproduced. Bhabha suggests that colonial authority is

390 हेमंत शर्मा (सं), भारतेन्दु समग्र, प्रचारक ग्रंथावली परियोजना, वाराणसी, तृतीय संस्करण, 1989, पृ.494

391 वही, पृ.496

392 William Shakespeare, ibid, p40

393 Quoted in Romila Thapar, The Past and Prejudice, NBT, Delhi, p12

rendered 'hybrid' and 'ambivalent' by this process of replication, thus opening up spaces for the colonized to subvert the master discourse."[394]

In its early phase, translations done in Hindi were mostly from Sanskrit, Bangla and English and whatever non-English literature was translated it was through English only. In this regard we may remember French Victor Hugo, Maurice Metrilunk, Moliere, Anatole France, Balzac, Alexander Duma and Maupassant, German Shiller, Lessing, Stephen Zweig, Goethe, Thomas Mann, Russian Tolstoy, Gorky, Turgenev, Spaniard Cervantes, Swedish legerlaph, Italian Moravia and so on.

But the situation changed when Madan Lal Madhu translated Turgenev's 'otasi ei deti' into Hindi(Pita aur Putra, Videshi Bhasha Prakashan Griha, Moscow, 1959) and Nirmal Verma Jan Otcenasek's 'Romeo Juli aatma'(Romeo Juliet aur Andhera, Rajkamal Prakashan, Delhi, 1964) for the first time directly from original Russian and Czech respectively. It can rightly be called a historical postcolonial moment in Hindi literature as for the first time we were able to negotiate by our own, without any colonial mediation or intervention.

Introducing fourteen stories of Carrel Chapek to Hindi reading public, Nirmal Verma declared: "unfortunately our interaction with central and east Europe has been very limited. Whatever little information we occasionally get that comes only through English——and that even very unsatisfactory and imbalanced. If

394 Ania Loomba, Colonialism/Post colonialism, Rutledge, London, New York, 1999, p89

we, for a moment take exception of Kafka, Mann, Rilke etc., then even in English the translation of so many important works could not be easily found. Anyway we are under the heavy influence of Anglo-American literature for past so many years that only through their window, we have been observing the art activities of Europe. It goes without saying that this window shows a very one-dimensional, and to some extant prejudiced view. This is the reason, till this date, we are more familiar of second or third rate Anglo-American writers than Musil, Hasek, Atila Joseph, Chapek or Karl Crass."[395]Later Nirmal Verma translated some more stories of Czeck writers such as Carrel Chapek(Carrel Chapek ki kahaniyaan, Rajkamal Prakashan, 1966) Milan Kundera (Itne bade Dhabbe) and so on. It is a fact to be highlighted that till that date Kundera is yet to be translated in English.

Nirmal starts his translation 'Romeo Juliet aur Andhera' with these words:

"पुराने घर पुराने लोगों की तरह होते हैं—स्मृतियों से भरे हुए। पुराने घरों की एक अपनी जिन्दगी, अपना चेहरा होता है। मानव-वास की शायद ही कोई गन्ध हो जिसे पुराने घरों की जर्जरित दीवारों ने अपने में जज्ब न किया हो।...पुराने मकानों की अपनी आवाजें भी हैं। सुनो: आँगन के उपर टँगी खुली गैलरी में कोई धीरे-धीरे जा रहा है, घिसटते, थके क़दमों से; अपने में ही धीरे-धीरे सीटी बजाता हुआ। अब वो ठहर गया है...माचिस की जलती तीली का प्रकाश दीवार पर सिमट आया...और वह फिर चलने लगा; एक अजीब उदास-सी गूँज आती है घिसी-पिटी पुरानी काठ की सीढियों से।"[396]

Nirmal's reader will recognize that they are listening Nirmal Verma, not Jan Otcenasek. This is complete appropriation – domesticating all the foreign elements of the text and making it, original-like.[397] In Hindi, it became a cliché and a parameter

395 Nirmal Verma, Karel Chapek ki Kahaniyaan, Rajkamal Prakashan, Delhi.1996

396 Yan otchenashek, Romeo Juliet aur Andhera, Rajkamal Paperbacks, 1984, p.5

397 Although Prasenjit Gupta had argued in his doctoral thesis that Nirmal's translations are "resistant, rough and foreignized, it is hardly convincing .see, Indian Errant, Indialog, Delhi, First Edition 2002

to appreciate a good translation by prefixing, 'as if it is originally written in Hindi'.

But his contemporary other postcolonial translator had adopted different methodology. In the preface of Anna Karenina's Hindi translation, Dr. Madan Lal Madhu proclaims: "I would only like to say about the translation of this Novel is that this is done not through English but from original Russian and Tolstoy' style is preserved avoiding literal translation. Tolstoy's style is generally complex since it is mostly contemplative and it seems as if joining bricks of ideas together he erects huge building of his main thought in the form of very long sentences. It is possible to convert these long sentences into small one and make it simple and fluent for Hindi reader but it may harm those thoughts and ideas of the great writer on which he wanted to emphasize or wanted to take it to its logical climax. That's why the Hindi reader should read it almost as Russian readers read it in Russian."[398] Here the translator is in favour of *Foreignizing*, instead of domesticating the text.

It can be argued that in comparison to *domesticated* texts, *Foreignizing* texts have more potentialities in evolving the language since it defamiliarizes the target language. So the translation which is faithful to the source is good for the health of the target language whereas domesticated translations may be showing the confidence of the target language but have no positive effect on it. Moreover both the responses can be traced in the fact of Post coloniality.[399]

398 Lev Tolstoy, Anna Karenina, Praogress Publication, Moscow, 1981

399 The Empire Writes Back argued that the term post-colonial might provide a different way of understanding colonial relation: no longer a simple binary opposition, black colonized vs. white colonizer; Third World vs. the West, but an engagement with all the varied manifestations of colonial power... "Bill Ashcroft, Gareth Griffiths and Helen Tiffin, The Empire Writes Back, Rutledge, London and New York, First Indian Reprint, 2005, p.200.

Bibliography

- A.K.Ramanujan, The interior Landscape, New York Review Books, New York, 1967
- A.K.Ramanujan, The interior Landscape, OUP, 1967
- A.Lawson & Tiffin, Describing Empire: Post colonialism and Textuality, Rutledge, London, 1994
- Acharya Vishveshwar, (ed.) Hindi Abhinavbharti, Delhi University, Delhi, 2nd edition 1973
- Andre lefevere, Translation, Rewriting & the Manipulation of Literary Fame, Routledge London &New York, First Published 1992
- Ania Loomba, Colonialism/Post colonialism, Rutledge, London, New York, 1999
- Annemarie Schimmel, *Classical Urdu Literature from the beginning to Iqbal*, Otto Hararassowitz. Wiesbaden, 1975
- Bharata-Muni, The Natyasastra, Tr, Manmohan Ghosh, Asiatic Society of Bengal, Calcutta, 1951
- Bill Ashcroft, Gareth Griffiths and Helen Tiffin, The Empire Writes Back, Rutledge, London and New York, First Indian Reprint, 2005
- Bipin Chandra Pal, *Memories of My Life and Times*, UBS Publishers. New Delhi, 2004

- Brian Gollnick, Approaches to Latin-American Literature, in (ed.) Philip Swanson, Arnold, London, 2003
- C.A. Bayly,) *The Local Roots of Indian Politics, 1880-1920.* Clarendon Press, Oxford, Great Britain, 1975
- C.S.Ranga Iyer, Father India, Selvyn & Blount Ltd, London, 1927
- Catherine B. Asher and Cynthia Talbot, India before Europe, Cambridge University Press, First South Asian Edition 2008
- Chandravati Lakhanpal, Mother India Ka Jawab, Gurukul Kangri, Dehradun, 1927
- Chandravati Lakhanpal, Striyon ki Sthiti, Ganga Pustak Karyalaya, Luchnow, 1934
- Charles Haliisey,(Tr.) Therigatha, Murti Classical library of India, Harvard University Press, Cambridge, Massachusetts, 2015
- Charulata Devi, The Fair Sex of India: A Reply to "Mother India", Ramakrishna Cottage, Calcutta, 1929
- Colin Gordon (ed.) Power/Knowledge Selected interviews and other writings, Michel Foucault, Pantheon Books, New york, 1980
- D.G.Mukherji, A Son of Mother India Answers, E.P.Dutton & Company, New York, U.S.A., 1928
- Daniel H. H. Ingalls (*translated*), An Anthology of Sanskrit Court Poetry, Vidyakar's Subhasitaratnakosh, Cambridge, Massachusetts, Harvard University Press, 1965

- Deborah Parsons, *Theorists of the Modernist Novel*, Routledge, London and New York, First Indian Reprint, 2015
- Deviprasad '*Munshif'(ed)* , Mahila Mriduvani, Nagri Pracharini Sabha, Varanasi, 1905
- Dharamveer Bharati (ed.&tr.) Deshantar, Bhartiya Jnanpith, Punarnava edition, Delhi, 2003
- Dharmaveer (ed.) Simantani Upadesh, Vani Prakashan, New Delhi; 1999
- Dhirendra Verma, Hindi Rashtra Ya Suba Hindustan, Leader Press, Allahabad, 1930
- Dipankar Gupta, Mistaken Modernity, Harper Collins Publishers India, Eight impression 2016
- Durga Prasad, *An English Translation of Satyarth Prakash*, Virjanand Press, Lahore, 1908
- Elzbieta Sklodowska, Latin American Literatures in The Companion to Latin American Studies, ed. Philip Swanson, Arnold publishers, London, 2003
- F.E Keay, A History of Hindi Literature, Asian Educational Services, New Delhi, Madras, Reprint 1989
- G.N.Devy, Indian Literary Criticism, Orient Blackswan, Hyderabad, 2014
- Ganga Prasad Singh, 'Visharad'(ed.), Hindi ke Musalmaan Kavi, Lahari Book Depot, Kashi, 1926
- George Abraham Grierson(ed.), Linguistic Survey of India, vol. vi, Central Printing Office, Govt. of India, Calcutta, 1904

- George Luzern Hurt, Poets of the Tamil Anthology, Princeton University Press, Princeton, New Jersy, 1979
- Girijadutt Shukla, Brajbhushan Shukla(eds.), Hindi Kavya ki Kokilayen, Sahitya-Mandir, Prayag, 1933
- Goswami Harirai, Shreenath ji ki Prakatya varta, Vidya Vibhag, Shreenathdwara, 1919
- H. Balasubrahmanyam, Prof. K. Nachimuttu (Hindi translation), Tolkappiyam, Dr. Central Institute of Classical Tamil, Chennai, First Edition, 2021
- Hardevi, 'Hindu Widows by one of them' in Journal of the National *Indian Association*, 121, 1881
- Hardevi, *Stree Vilap*. Arya Darpan Press, Shahjahanpur, UP, 1881
- Hazariprasad Dwivedi, Hindi Sahitya: Udbhav aur Vikas, Rajkamal Prakashan, Delhi. Reprint 1995
- Henry Beveridge(ed.), Tuzuk-i-Jahangiri or Memoirs of Jahangir, Translated by Alexander Rogers, Royal Asiatic Society, London, 1909-1914
- J. L. Austin, How to Do Things with Words, OUP, 1962
- James Mill, The History of British India, Pasternoster Row, Baldwin, London 1817
- Jane Gonda (Editor), A History of Indian Literature, The Relation between Tamil and Classical Sanskrit Literature, Otto Harasowicz, Wiesbaden, Volume 10, 1976
- Jawaharlal Nehru, An Autobiography, Oxford University Press, New Delhi, Fifth Impression, 1987

- Jeremy Tambling, Madmen and other survivors, Reading Lu Xun's Fiction, Hong Kong University Press, Aberdeem, Hong kong, 2007
- John Murdoch (compiled), Catalogue of the Christian vernacular literature of India, Caleb Foster Press, Madras, 1870
- John Oliver Perry(ed.), Voices of Emergency, Popular Prakashan, Bombay, First published, 1983
- John Stratton Hawley, Three Bhakti Voices,(Mirabai, Surdas, and Kabīr in their Time and Ours), Oxford University Press 2005
- Julia Lovell (tr.), The Real Story of A Q , Penguin Books, 2009
- Jyoti Prasad Mishra 'Nirmal'(ed).Stree Kavita Kaumodi, Gandhi Hindi Pustak Bhandar, Prayag, 1931
- K. Kailashpati, Tamil Heroic Poetry, Clarendon Press, Oxford, 1968,
- K. Kailashpati, Tamil Heroic Poetry, Clarendon Press, Oxford, 1968
- K.Natrajan, Miss Mayo's Mother India: A Rejoinder, G.A.Natesan & Co.Madras, 1927
- K.W. Jones, *Arya Dharm Hindu Consciousness in 19th –Century Punjab,* Manohar Publishers and Distributors, *Delhi,* 2006
- Kamil Václav Zvelebil, The Smile of Murugan, E.G. Bill, Leiden, Netherlands, 1973
- Karen Pechilis Prentiss, The Embodiment of Bhakti, Oxford University Press, New York Oxford 1999

- Kishoridas Vajpayee, Hindi Shabdanushaasan, Nagri Pracharini Sabha, Varanasi, 4th edition 1988
- Kishorilal Gupta, Saroj Sarvekchan, Hindustani Akademi, Allahabad, first edition 1967
- Kumkum Sangari, Suresh Vaid, (ed.), *Recasting Women*, Kali for Women, New Delhi, Reprint 1993
- Lala Bhagvandin (ed.), Aalam-Keli, Umashankar Mehta, Ram Ghat, Kashi, 1922
- Lala Bhagwan Din,(ed.) Aalam Keli, Umashankar Mehta Publication, Ramghat, Kashi, 1922
- Lala Lajpat Rai, Unhappy India, Banna Publishing Co. Calcutta, 1928
- Lata Mani, Contentious Tradition in Recasting Women, Kumkum Sangari, Suresh Vaid,(eds.), Kali for Women, New Delhi, Reprinted 1993
- Lucy Carol Stout, *The Hindustani Kayastha: The Kayastha Pathshala, and the Kayastha Conference, 1873-1914*, University of California , Berkeley, 1976
- Ludwik Sternbach, A Descriptive Catalogue of Poets quoted in Sanskrit Anthologies and Inscriptions, Otto Harasowicz, Wiesbaden, 1978
- Ludwik Sternbach, Subhasita, Gnomic and Didactic Literature, Otto Harasowicz, Wiesbaden 1974
- M. Jacqui Alexander and Chandra Talpade Mohanty,(eds.) Feminist Genealogies, Colonial Legacies, Democratic Futures, Routledge, London & New York, 1997

- M. Kaur, *Role of Women in the Freedom Movement, 1857-1947.* Sterling Publishers, New Delhi, 1968
- M.Singh, History and Culture of Punjab, Atlantic Publishers and distributors. New Delhi, 1989
- Maitrayee Chaudhuri, Feminism in India: The Tales and its Telling, Revue Tiers Monde, No. 209, FÉMINISMES DÉCOLONIAUX, GENRE ETDÉVELOPPEMENT (janvier-mars 2012), Publications de la Sorbonne,
- Mangla Anuja, Patrakarita ke yug nirmata Hemantkumari Devi Chaudhari, Prabhat Prakashan, Delhi, 2010
- Manoranjan Jha, Katherine Mayo and India, People's Publishing House, New Delhi, 1971
- Margaret Macnicol, Poems by Indian Women, Oxford University Press, 1923
- Mark Currie (Edited and Introduced), Metafiction, Routledge, 2013
- Mark Wollaeger and Matt Eatough, *(ed)* The Oxford Handbook of Global Modernisms, Oxford University Press, 2018
- McNeill, Andrew, (Ed) , T*he Essays of Virginia Woolf. Volume 4: 1925 to 1928.*, The Hogarth Press, London, 1984
- Michel Foucault, Discipline and Punish: The Birth of the Prison, Vintage Books, New York, 1979
- Michel Foucault, Madness and civilization, Vintage Books Edition, New York, 1988
- Milan Kundera, *The Art of Novel*, Faber and Faber, London Boston, 1988

- Minna G.Cowan, The Education of the Women of India, Fleming H. Revell Company, New York Chicago Toronto, 1912
- Mishrabandhu Vinod, part I, Ganga Pustak Mala Karyalaya, Lucknow, 2nd Edition, 1927
- Mishrabandhu Vinod, Part ii, Ganga Pustak Mala Karyalaya, Lucknow, 2nd Edition, 1927
- Mohammad Sadiq, A History of Urdu Literature, Oxford University Press, Madras Calcutta Bombay, 1964
- Mrinalini Sinha (ed.) Selection from Mother India, Kali for Women Press, New Delhi, 1998
- N. Gerald Barrier, BANNED Controversial Literature and Political Control in British India1907-1947, Manohar, Delhi, 2023
- N.K.Bhagwat(ed.), Therigatha or Pourings in verse of the Buddhist Bhikkhunis, Bombay University Publications, 1956
- Nazir Ahmad, Kitab-i-Nauras,(ed.), Sangeet Natak Akadami, 1956
- Nemichandra Jain(ed.), Muktibodh rachnavali, Rajkamal Paperbacks, Delhi, First edition, 1985
- Nirmal Verma, Kala ka Jokhim, Rajkamal Prakashan, Delhi, 2nd Edition, 1984
- Norbert Krapf (edited & translated) Beneath the Cherry Sapling: Legends from Franconia, Fordham University, 1988
- P.V.Kane, History of Sanskrit Poetics, Motilal Banarasidas, New, New, Delhi, Reprint 2002

- P.V.Naganatha Sastry(ed), Kavyalankar of Bhamaha, Motilal Banarasidas, New, New, New, New, Delhi, Reprint1991
- Padmanji B. *Yamunaparyatan*. Snehvardhan Prakashan, Pune, 2005
- Partha Chatterjee, *Empire & Nation*, Permanent Black, Ranikhet, First Paperback Edition 2012
- Partha Chatterjee, *The Nationalist Resolution of the Women's Question, in Empire & Nation*, Permanent Black, Ranikhet, First Paperback Printing 2012
- People's Linguistic Survey of India, Vol.one , Orient Blacks Swan Pvt.Ltd. Delhi, First published, 2014
- Prasenjit Gupta, Indian Errant, Indialog, Delhi, First Edition 2002
- R. Raj Singh, Bhakti and Philosophy, Lexington Books, Lanham, 2006
- Radha Kumar, The History of Doing, Zubaan, Delhi, First Published 1993
- Ram Ratan Bhatnagar, The Rise and Growth of Hindi Journalism, , Kitab Mahal, Allahabad, 1947
- Ramabai, *The High Caste Hindu Woman*, Fleming H. Revell Company, New York, Chicago Toronto: 1901
- Ramchandra Shukla, Hindi Sahity ka Itihas, Nagri Pracharini Sabha, Varansi, 20th Reprint, 1983
- Rammurti Tripathi, Ardhashati ka Bhartiya Kavya-chintan:vipaksha, aur pakshsa, Vani Prakashan, Delhi, 2000

- Ramniranjan Parimalendu(ed.)Khadi Boli ka Padya, Sahitya Akademi, First edition, 2008
- Ramvilas Sharma, Bhartendu Yug, Vinod Pustak Mandir, Agra, 1956
- Ramvilas Sharma, Bhasha aur Samaj, People's Publishing House, Delhi, 1956
- Ramvilas Sharma, Mahavir Prasad Dwivedi aur Hindi Navjagran, Rajkamal Prakashan Delhi, First Edition, 1977
- Ranjit Guha, On Some Aspects of the Historiography of Colonial India, Subaltern Studies I , OUP, Delhi, 1982
- Raza Mir, Ali Husain Mir, Anthems of Resistance, Indialink, Roli Books, New Delhi, 2006
- Romila Thapar, The Past and Prejudice, NBT, Delhi,
- Ronald Taylor(edited and translated), Aesthetics and politics, Verso, London, 1980, p.162
- S. N. Dasgupta and , S.K.De ,.A History of Sanskrit Literature, Calcutta University Press, 1947
- S.K.De, History of Sanskrit Poetics, Farma KLM Private Limited, Calcutta.2nd edition 1960
- S.V.Subrahamanium, Tolkappiyam in English , Meiyappan Publishing House, Chidambaram, first edition 2004
- Sachchidanand Vatsyayan, Adyatan, Saraswati Vihar, Delhi, Second Edition 1978
- Sant Nihal Singh 'A Long Distance Intellectual Companion' in *Sachchidananda Sinha Commemoration Volume* Patna: The United Press LTD, 1947

- Satya P. Mohanty(ed), Colonialism Modernity and Literature, orient black Swan, Delhi, 2011
- Savitri Sinha , Madhyakalin Hindi Kaviyatriyan, , Aatmaram and sons, Delhi, First Edition 1953
- Selected Poetry of Amiri Baraka/Le Roi Jones, William Morrow & Co, New York, 1979
- Shantaram Ganpatrau Warty, Sister India, Sister India Office, Bombay, 1928
- Shitikanth Mishra, Khari Boli Ka Andolan, Kashi Nagri Pracharini Sabha, Varanasi, 1956
- Shobhana Nijhawan, Women and Girls in the Hindi Public Sphere: Periodical Literature in Colonial North India, Oxford University Press, First Published 2012
- Shyama Prasad Ganguly, Meenakshi Sundriyal, (Ed & Tr.), ... yeh Sampannata Bikhari Hui, Sahitya Akademi & Grulac, First Edition 2006
- Sigmund Freud, Case Histories II, The Pelican Freud Library, Vol.9, Penguin Books, 1979
- Sisir Kumar Das , A History of Indian Literature, vol.viii, Sāhitya Akademi, New Delhi, Reprint 1991
- Sisir Kumar Das, Sahibs and Munshis, Papyrus, Calcutta, Reprint 2001
- Sri Vyathit Hridaya(ed), Hindi Kavya ki Kalamayee Tarikayen, Pramod Pustak Mala, Katara, Prayag, Jan1941
- Sudha Chauhan, Mila Tej se Tej, Hans Prakashan, Allahabad, 1975

- Sudhir Chandra, Enslaved Daughters Colonialism, Law and Women's Rights, Oxford University Press, New Delhi, 2008.
- Suman Raje, Hindi Sahitya ka Aādhā Itihash, Bhartiya Gyanpith, Delhi, Third Edition 2006
- Sushie Tharu and K.Lalita(eds)Women Writing in India, OUP, 1993
- Sushil Kumar Tiwari(compilation), Poems and Songs on Azad Hind Fauj &Subhash Chandra Bose, IGNOU, New Delhi, 2023
- Susnigdha Dey, Spanish Literature ; Aspects & Appraisal, B.R.Publishing Corporation, Delhi, 1991
- Swami Gokulnath, Bhāva-Siṃdhu, Lallu Bhai Chhagan Lal Desai, Ahmadabad, second edition 1936
- Swamini Atmaprajnananda Saraswati, Rsikas of the Rigveda, D.K Printworld Delhi, first published 2013
- T.Grahame Bailey History of Urdu Literature, Oxford University Press, London, 1932, p.20
- T.S.Eliot, *The sacred wood*, Faber and Faber, London, 1920
- T.S.Eliot, Tradition and individual Talent in D.J.Enright, Ernst De Chickera (ed), English Critical Text, Oxford University Press, 2001
- Takanobu Takahashi, Tamil Love Poetry and Poetics, E.G. Brill, Leiden, New York, Conn., 1995
- Tharu S. &Lalita K, *Women Writing in India* Delhi: Oxford University Press, 1991

- The Reception and Rendition of Freud in China: China's Freudian Slip, (ed.) Tao Jiang, Philip J. Ivanhoe, Routledge, First Published, 2013
- The True Story of Ah Q, Yang Hsien-yi & Gladys Yang (Tr.), Foreign Languages Press, Peking, 1953
- Theodor Adorno and Max Horkheimer, Dialectics of Enlightenment, Verso, London, 1994
- Tzvetan Todorov, The Origin of Genres in Modern Genre Theory, David Duff (ed.) Routledge, 2000
- Uma Nehru, Miss Mayo ki Mother India (Sachitra Hindi Anuvaad) , Hindustan Press, Allahabad, 1928
- V.D.Mahajan, Modern Indian Political Thought. S.Chand & Company , New Delhi, 1987
- V.S.Mall (edit) Pratapnarayan-Granthavali, Nagari Pracharini Sabha, Varanasi, 1992
- V.S.Sukthankar, Ghate's lectures on Rigveda, Oriental Book Agency, Poona, Revised and enlarged second edition, 1926
- Victor Kiernan(Tr.), Poems by Faiz, Vanguard Books, London, 1971
- Vidya Dhar Mahajan, Modern Indian Political Thought, S.Chand & Company, New Delhi, First Edition 1987
- Vidyanivas Mishra(ed), Aalam Granthāvalī, Vani Prakashan, Delhi, 2000
- Vijayshankar Srivastava,(ed), Cultural Contours of India, Abhinav Publications, Delhi, 1987

- Vishalakshi Menon, Indian Women and Nationalism, The UP Story, Shakti Books, New Delhi, 2003
- Vishnu Prabhakar, Rameshchandra Shah(eds)Prasad Rachna-Sanchayan, Sahitya Akademi, Delhi, 2010
- Vishwanath Prasad Mishra, Hindi Sahitya ka Atit, Vani Prakashan, Delhi, 2014
- Willett, John (ed. and trans.). Brecht on Theatre, Eyre Methuen, London, 2001
- William A.Lyell, Jr., Lu Hsun's Vision of Reality, University of California Press, Berkeley, 2022
- William Shakespeare, The Merchant of Venice, Macmillan India ltd., 2008
- Yang Hsein-hi and Gladys Yang,(tr.) *Selected Stories of Lu Xun,* Oriole Editions, New York, 1972

Journals

- Economic and Political Weekly , Jun. 9, 1973, Vol. 8, No. 23, Jun. 9, 1973
- Economic and Political Weekly, Vol. 35, No. 15, April, 27, 1991
- Forum for Modern Language Studies. (1993) Vol. xxxix No. 1,
- Gender & History, Vol.29 No.2 August 2017,
- History of Religions, Vol. 14, No. 2, Nov., 1974
- Indian Literature, Vol. 32, No. 5 (133), September-October, 1989

- Indian Literature, Vol. 53, No. 5 (253), September/October 2009
- Indian Literature, vol. 53, no. 5 (253), 2009
- International Journal of Hindu Studies, world heritage press, vol.4, april 2000
- Modern Asian Studies, Vol. 38, No. 2, May, 2004
- Modern Chinese Literature and Culture, Vol. 23, No. 1, Special Issue on Discourses of Disease, Spring, 2011
- Seminar, Annual No. 221, Delhi, Jan 1978
- The American Historical Review, Vol. 116, No. 3, June 2011
- The Englishwoman's Review of Social and Industrial Questions, : Rutledge, London, 1902
- The Hindustan Review, Allahabad, The Indian Press, 1906,
- The Indian Magazine and Review. 1892
- The Indian Magazine, Kegan Paul, Trench & Co. London, 1886, 1887 and 1889
- The Journal of American Folklore, Vol. 84, No. 331
- The Nineteenth Century, XX:364-372 , 1886
- Victorian Studies, vol.14, No.4, June 1971

World Wide Web:

- http: //www .encyclopedia. com
- http://en.wikipedia.org/wiki/Claude_Eatherly

- http://indiainbusiness.nic.in/newdesign/
- http://indiasportstv.blogspot.in
- http://scroll.in/article/667570
- http://www.academia.edu/377215/Cultural_imperialism_or_vernacular_modernity_Hindi_newspapers_in_a_globalizing_India
- http://www.indiaspend.com/cover-story/hindi-outpaces-english-globally-linguistic-survey-68309
- http://www.jstor.org/stable/4358239
- http://www.nybooks.com
- https://stateofnationalism.eu/article/culturalnationalism
- http://www.thelibrarypk.com/tareekh-e-farishta/
- https://en.wikipedia.org/wiki/Cannibalism in China
- https://frontline.thehindu.com/columns/K_Satchidanandan/dilemmas-of-indian-literary-criticism/
- https://indianhistorycollective.com
- https://www.apnimaati.com
- https://www.britannica.com/art/fiction-literature
- https://www.firstthings.com/blogs/leithart/2005/05/renaissance-and-modernity
- https://www.hindikavita.com
- https://www.jstor.org/stable/23593740, https://www.pgurus.com/dr-nagaswamy-reveals-how-tholkappiyam-follows-bharata-sastra-and-how-carnatic-music-got-its-name/

- https://www.youtube.com/watch?v=bKzmYHfCWmo)
- https://www.youtube.com/watch?v=qpgQzoeZQhU https://www.youtube.com/watch?v=0-DEILfO3iM)

www.ingramcontent.com/pod-product-compliance
Lightning Source LLC
LaVergne TN
LVHW021152160826
845679LV00024B/2095

* 9 7 9 8 8 9 6 1 0 9 4 8 8 *